"I am mesmerized with the contents of the book. Unforgettable and fascinating details; very sensitive and frank revelations. The violence and atrocities towards women are prevalent like a virus across the society. The book moved me to tears. Kudos to Dr Latha, for bringing this into public domain."

Alka Suri, Director, DESIDOC, DRDO, N. Delhi

"Christie's book not only highlights the problem that the woman faces but also provides for them a platform to get back to society with dignity, hope and celebrate their role as a woman. Reading this book will inspire every reader to honour the woman whom God has created in His image and will change our perspective. It is a book that echoes the pain of millions waiting to live a life of freedom. Her commitment to God and her passion to serve people is reflected in this book."

Rev Benjamin C A, National Director,
FEBA INDIA, Bangalore

"Dr Latha uses case studies to provide understanding on how abuse starts, becomes stealthy and vicious and finally locks the victim into silence and devastating inner turmoil. She explores the difficult question of why people who abuse also claim to love their victims and discusses the helplessness of family members who find themselves helpless to intervene. She highlights the slow loss of identity and spontaneity in the lives of abused wives and the horror and helplessness of their children. The book has a message of hope written through its pages, for those who have reached the end of hope, calling couples who live with abuse to seek counseling and marriage therapy and to believe that God can bring

restoration. I believe that this book will highlight the need for many abused wives to break the silence and never to believe that they should be blamed for wife battering."

Gladys K Mwiti, PhD Consulting Clinical Psychologist, Founder & CEO | Oasis Africa - Center for Transformational Psychology & Trauma, Nairobi, Kenya

"This book is another rich resource for those who either suffer in, or serve people in desperately needy situations. It is bound to shed light, bring comfort and strength to the many that are undergoing the despair and pain of abuse in the family. The stories and insights gathered through the many personal interactions will surely bless the reader."

Dr Jacob Cherian, Professor of NT and Dean of Faculty at Center for Global Leadership Development, Bangalore, India

"Dr Latha has written a compelling and sensitive description of the terrible dilemma of how evil has come into what God has intended to be the most sacred of relationships. It is full of real life examples, accompanied by thoughtful counsel. Abuse affronts our very human dignity and robs the vulnerable among us of happiness, security and self esteem. She describes a sure path to healing and hope - not a fairy tale but Truth and Love personified. I commend this book as a much needed guide for women who are trapped in the cycle of abuse. It will save your life. It will give you a path forward and a hope for the future."

Jerry E. White, PhD, Author and Speaker, Retired US Air Force Major General, International President Emeritus, The Navigators

"This is a brave, honest and deeply felt work about abuse in marriage. It will help many couples, particularly women, fight back from a disadvantaged situation and rebuild their lives."

Dr Kavery Nambisan, Surgeon and Novelist

"Dr. Christie awakens us to the reality of domestic violence and the stories show how so many women are being subjected to repeated abuse within their own home. This book is not just a collection of stories but a handbook for women facing marital abuse. It voices out what a woman goes through physically, emotionally and spiritually while facing abuse. The best part is that there is always hope. An abusive relationship does not have to end your life. I hope this book finds its way into the hands of those caught in the web of such abuse and gives them the courage to rise above it, the courage to seek help and not stay silent. And I hope that many men will rise up to feel this passionately about women's safety!"

Kavitha Emmanuel, Founder Director, Women of Worth (WOW), Founder of the 'Dark is beautiful' & 'Girl Arise' campaigns

"Dr. Christie has tackled with insight, compassion and courage the deeply pervasive worldwide problem of women and child abuse. She brings into scorching light a problem of agonizing pain & sadness which most marriages try to keep hidden in darkness & subterfuge. She not only exposes the depth & extent of the problem, but gives very practical counsel as to the Way Out. Over & above her psychological understandings, she even shows how faith in Christ & sustained prayer can make a mighty difference. This is a book of required reading for all. Bravo, Dr. Christie! You have rendered humankind a beautiful service with this deep, tender & sensitively written volume of healing. May it be very widely read."

Michael Cassidy, *Founder of African Enterprise,*
& Hon Co-Chair of the Lausanne Movement

"Dr Latha Christie's driving desire to make clear what domestic violence is all about and thereby give hope and healing to women is commendable. She describes real life experiences, document attested facts, and firmly couches these within her deep commitment to the Christian faith. Dr. Christie's book will add a significant part in empowering women to stand up for their rights and the practical advice she gives will certainly guide them towards dignity, self respect and desire for living, they have sadly been deprived of. Her's is an inspired confident message "Dare to dream... everything is possible with God.""

Dr Ken Gnanakan, *Speaker and Author, Chairman,*
International Council of Higher Education, Chancellor, Acts Group,
Chairman & Managing Director, Theological Book Trust.

"This book is well researched and well written. It is based on the firsthand experience of a large number of women, who ironically experienced violence in the very places where they should have felt safe. It serves as an eye opener and a guide to victims of domestic violence such that they do not remain victims, but emerge as victors and rediscover hope and "beauty from the ashes." I strongly recommend the book to not just women but anyone who intends to understand the causes & the remedies of this malaise that affects reportedly 40% of marriages in the country."

Dr Prateep V Philip, *IPS,*
ADGP Economic Offences Wing, TN

"Dr Latha Christie has reflected deep sense of understanding of the current and burning issues of present society. Her contribution to the betterment of women in particular is immense and noble. The book is highly informative; reveals the emotional turmoil, the hurt, humiliation, agony and despair and clearly elucidates the emotions and feelings of victims. It helps one to understand the root cause of the problem and gives practical ways to deal with it and is for all those who work for women empowerment."

Dr K Ramachandran, Director, Defence Institute of Psychological Research, DRDO, Delhi

"The book is a bold, heart-wrenching account that makes for compelling reading on the brutality of marital abuse and the havoc it causes. The combination of personal experience with case studies, statistics, and scholarly references, enhances the value of the book for the reader. It shows the widespread prevalence of abuse which cuts across geography, class, and culture. Dr Christie offers hope to women in similar situations by showing how to combat and emerge out of a seemingly hopeless plight."

Saleem Peeradina, Author and Poet, Emeritus Professor, Siena Heights University, USA

"Dr. Latha has produced a wonderful blend of heart-wrenching experience and practical advice for the women who are caught in a trap where it seems there are no options to domestic violence except suicide. I am personally aware of children orphaned in India because their mothers saw no other way out. We have provided batterer intervention programs for almost 20 years and the stories in this book are very much like those I have heard from my clients, but the

good news is that there is hope in Jesus Christ. We have seen many marriages saved and many batterers changed. It is my hope that this book will be widely read and distributed in India and, as a result, many lives and marriages will be saved."

Dr Troy Reiner, Director of Word of Life Counseling Center and Counseling Training Institute, Wichita, Kansas, USA

WHEN THE FLAME FLICKERS

WHEN THE FLAME FLICKERS

Emerging from Marital Abuse

LATHA CHRISTIE

RESOURCE *Publications* · Eugene, Oregon

Resource Publications
A division of Wipf and Stock Publishers
199 W 8th Ave, Suite 3
Eugene, OR 97401

When the Flame Flickers
By Christie, Latha
Copyright©2015 SAIACS
ISBN 13: 978-1-5326-7751-9
Publication date 12/11/2018
Previously published by SAIACS, 2015

Table of Contents

Dedication

I gladly dedicate this book to my lovely sons,
Pradeep and Praveen:
without them, this would have never happened.

Foreword

A constant contribution to the upliftment of others is one of the things that has driven and sustained me throughout my life, and perhaps this, combined with my drive for social justice, made me step beyond the traditional role assigned to women and become the first Indian lady IPS officer way back in 1972. I believe that engaging in social issues and understanding injustice should make us angry, and this anger should be channeled into positive action. This belief made me choose "Drug Abuse and Domestic Violence" as the subject of my PhD, which I completed during my active service in the Indian Police. Even after my retirement from the post of Director General of India's Bureau of Police Research and Development, my main motto has been to help underprivileged women and children whose tears go unnoticed.

In the present Indian scenario, seeing the prevalent cruelties towards girls and women, it is the duty of every Indian to confront the issues that make women vulnerable. Intimate partner abuse is one such issue. Now and then, newspapers report stories of crime against women perpetuated by the husband. These men often claim to love the victim but then subjugate her and make her fully dependent on them, so that she does not talk of the abuse to anybody, thinking at all times that she is the one at fault. I sympathize with such women. Abuse does not happen far from you. It happens in your neighborhood, in the homes of your colleagues, friends or maids. Dr Latha Christie's book *"When the Flame Flickers: Emerging From Marital Abuse"* is an accurate, intelligent and articulate treatment of the subject of abuse. Latha Christie, a senior scientist in Defense and a PhD from the Indian Institute of Science, Bangalore, has eruditely examined the most complicated subject of intimate partner abuse, with a matchless ability to bridge the worlds of theory and practice. She has penned this book with compassion and the drive to pursue the right path for a bigger and higher purpose. She has wrestled with the issue of divorce, which many prefer to avoid. In her clear and strong voice of conviction, she penetrates the curtain of confusion, shame and silence.

Women who are abused often wish to speak to someone who understands them and appreciate their pain and confusion. This book will serve as a handy tool for those who want to talk with a woman who has been there and has come out beautiful from the abuse. There may be others who want to read to understand what is happening in the lives of their loved ones. Many might be confused about whether what they are undergoing is abuse or some obsessive behavior of their spouse. You may be a victim of abuse, or browsing through this book in a bookstore. I welcome you to the pages of this book, which will take you on a journey of understanding one of the most misunderstood and most ignored subjects of our time. This book is filled with inspirational and practical insights on how one can still make one's life beautiful even after having been entangled in a life of abuse, and I encourage you to read it with expectation.

Women, whose stories you will read in this book, became aware of their rights and mustered up courage to come out of abuse, and motivate other women to come out of exploitation and suffering. The healing process detailed gives women the self-esteem to become self-respecting human beings. This unique book attempts to answer the following questions: Why are some men abusive? Do their upbringing and their life experiences, especially as children, play a role in them developing into an abuser? Are they able to break free from being an abuser, and if so, how? Why does a woman, who is in an abusive relationship, stay in the relationship, and why does she tend to move from one abusive relationship to another? Do any events in her childhood influence her choice not to leave? How does a woman deal with divorce after an abusive relationship? Is there any hope of healing an abusive relationship? And if so, how does one go about making the necessary changes? All of these questions and many more are addressed in this book, not only with skill but also with a refreshing honesty. This book has been written with a mission to draw victims back into the mainstream and lead them to the source of a new life governed by dignity, self-respect and deserved joy. The author has penned the different laps of this significant journey through the wilderness, in a narrative that is bound to bring millions of women in this country to the crossroad of choice, and beyond that, to the road to serenity, peace and a future filled with divine promise. Going through this manuscript left me with a feeling of encouragement that there is hope for the abused woman. Thank God for Latha's clarity of vision. I am happy to contribute this word of grateful appreciation to this book.

Dr Kiran Bedi,
Indian Police Service
56, Basement, Uday Park
New Delhi - 110049

Introduction

*H*istory has left us with strange views on how men are supposedly superior to the fairer sex. Indian society has been one of the more staunch advocates of this thought. *"Pati baghwan hai"* was a repeated chant in more than a few households and the deification of men has been sustained over time, regardless of religious background. Such beliefs have done Indian society untold damage, one of which is abuse within marriage.

History has always been what it was. That cannot be changed. But a legacy can be left behind, one of freedom and safety. The bizarre idea that women were created inferior has to be laid on the table, dissected, and analyzed, before diagnosis and healing of the sickness can begin.

I have written this book with a determination to bring clarity to what "Domestic Violence" really is, and to give hope and healing to women who have been broken by such atrocities within the walls of their own homes. The burning desire behind writing this book is to lead victims of this kind of abuse away from the shadows and to help them rebuild that which was destroyed: dignity, self-respect and a desire for life.

People tend to easily confide in me. I don't know why. They have said that my "…kind eyes, ability to listen patiently," puts them at ease. As they pour out their woes and closely guarded secrets to me, I can't help but listen and accept the role of a confidante.

My most treasured memory is of a woman telling me that she came to me because I had seemed to understand intuitively, all that she had confided in me, and that she could see that I had a deep longing to help her. She was right. I long to help women like her. I do not know where this empathy comes from; maybe some resonance with my distant past? I want to make a difference in the lives of as many women as I can reach, and I believe more and more women are being sent my way, by an unseen hand.

IN THE YEAR 2017 ALONE, 50,000 WOMEN WORLDWIDE WERE KILLED BY INTIMATE PARTNERS OR FAMILY MEMBERS

All of life is a tapestry. The coming together of this beautifully woven creation depends on every twist and turn the thread is forced to take. Behind the originality of this work of art is a Master Craftsman. He makes every thread of experience and every turn of events count in the long run. This book is written under the direction of this Master Craftsman.

The 2016 data from the National Crime Report Bureau, India, indicate that crimes against women have recorded a whopping 83% increase from 2007 to 2016; and there has been a 45% rise in incidences of 'Cruelty by Husband or his Relatives' (Sec 498A). A global study by the United Nations Office on Drugs and Crime (UNODC) says that in the year 2017 alone, 50,000 women worldwide were killed by intimate partners or family members—a figure that translates to 1.3

out of every 100,000 women. The same report also says that in India alone during that year, about 7,000 women were killed for dowry-related disputes. All this occurs despite the fact that there are many laws in most of the countries, including India which are supposed to protect women from domestic abuse.

The time has come for us to stop being uninvolved spectators to the abuse of women and to begin fighting for those of our sisters who are caught in the mesh of every kind of violence. It is the silence of the "good" that perpetuates such violence. Martin Luther King, Jr. said, "The ultimate tragedy is not the oppression and cruelty by the bad people but the silence over that by the good people." It is time we spoke out.

When violence against women are spoken about, many wonders why not violence against men? A special report by US Department of Justice says that 1 in 4 women and 1 in 9 men experience severe intimate partner physical violence, intimate partner sexual violence, and intimate partner stalking with impacts such as injury, fearfulness, post-traumatic stress disorder, use of victim services, and, contraction of sexually transmitted diseases [1]. Men do face domestic abuse. The dynamics of that abuse are mainly similar to that of women, but men may also suffer from shame, embarrassment and social stigma that they are not able to protect themselves. There is also, a fear that they may be falsely arrested and removed from their homes because of the assumption that they must be the perpetrator and not a victim because they are male and strong. Nevertheless, abuse by men against women is the most common form of intimate partner violence. So the main focus of this book is on women as victims and survivors who emerge victoriously and, without denying the horror of abuse of men, I have concentrated on the abuse of women.

Every experience narrated and every case study featured in this book *"When the Flame Flickers"* has emerged from the real lives of many wonderful women. Despite the horribly abusive situations that made the flame flicker, sometimes even snuffing it out, the spirit, the passion, and the determination these women possessed, helped them not only survive but rise out of the ashes like a phoenix, and move forward to create better lives for themselves and their kin. The metaphorical "flame" is the very essence of life that they refused to surrender, the life-spirit every human being needs to thrive. Many of them have actually asked for their names to be mentioned here. But, as much as I applaud their bravery, such exposure inevitably comes at an awful cost.

Dear Reader, if you find that you are not a woman who has faced abuse within her own home, please hand this book over to someone who fits the above description, once you are done reading this book.

If you happen to be one of those men who abuses his wife, in whatever form or in however violent a manner, please be advised that what you do is not natural. There is so much more that you can be—a loyal husband, a faithful friend, a chivalrous gentleman—the possibilities are endless. The source of the happiness you want lies in giving of yourself to your family and in protecting and nurturing life.I hope and pray that this book that you are holding in your hand will help you towards that journey of change.

Latha Christie

CURTAIN RAISER

The Letter

"As painful as it is to admit that we are being abused, it is even more painful to come to the conclusion that the person we love is someone we cannot afford to be around."
— *Anonymous*

She didn't know why she did that. This letter needed to be written. Or else, she would die with no one knowing the truth. She tried again.

Dearest Amma,

It's time you knew. I love you. I am so sorry.

You were always right.

Now, that wasn't so bad, she decided. As Indian as she was, she felt the need to speak those intimate words, to the woman who bore her, one last time. Tears began to fill her eyes and she breathed in deep. "Write, write, write," she chanted to herself, as she picked up the pen.

By the time you read this, I will have died. I woke up to a nightmare which has lasted ten years. I want out. I don't want you to hurt because of me. If there was any other way, any other option, I would have chosen it.

There isn't.

She didn't know when the tears had started flowing down her cheeks. She swiped at them and realized her hands were shaking.

It's all a dark, ugly lie. This marriage is no paradise, ammee. It's a hell hole. Amma, remember the doubts you had about Arpit?

A mother's instinct is NEVER wrong. How could I have known I was going to marry a sadistic monster? If only someone had warned me about who he really was…

She heard herself whimper. In a fit of rage at her prolonged weakness, she slapped herself hard. The power packed into that venomous blow surprised her. Her thumbnail cut the bridge of her nose in the process, and she ended up stabbing the inside of her eye. She sobbed softly as she tore at the paper with her pen.

> *Listening to you eulogize Arpit to Shantamma last week made me want to scream. You know what you said!?!*
>
> *You said, "I feel so sorry I ever doubted my son-in-law.*
>
> *Arpit has been such a good husband to our Lily. He fills her life with such good, good things and he..."*

Finally, she screamed. The neighbors at the other end of the street could have heard her but she no longer cared. For the first time in years, she let herself tear at her hair and wail like the life within her was leaving. She sobbed violently as her shoulders heaved and her pain emptied out into a wet puddle of tears on her bathroom floor. She couldn't remember how she had gotten there. Exhaustion came over her suddenly. She gave into it and shivered on the cold floor. Her head ached from all the crying. Lily wrapped her arms around herself and closed her eyes, wishing death would find her before she went looking for it.

Cobwebs. Too many of those silken entrapments hung suspended from the bathroom ceiling. The softness of the slight threads belied their deadly purpose. Surprisingly, they sparkled in the sunlight, streaming in through the high window. They were beautiful.

The steady outpouring of thoughts on cobwebs and abuse pounded against her head, as she lay there stretched out on the tiled bathroom floor. The cold floor soothed her sadness, for a little while. She lay there and thought through her plan of action. To kill or not to kill…oneself.

She sat up slowly and her head broke open into a migraine. An old friend. It had become as familiar to her as her own heartbeat. Like a hangover, every night after she had cried herself to sleep, she would wake in the morning and break open again. She got up very carefully and moved to the table, as if in a trance. The words from yesterday lay flat on the paper. They had no life; only blunt facts.

It was not the familiarity of abuse that had driven her to the edge. It was the taunting of old, unspoken dreams. With that realization, she lifted her pen one last time, to tell her story.

~~∞⊰⊹⊱∞~~

Amma,

I wondered if I had seen the signs. Or if I had only seen what I had wanted to see. The handsome and charming Arpit, who was the heartthrob of the entire college; the possessive boyfriend who had wanted me all to himself, so much so that I had to cut myself off from all my friends; the future son-in-law who wormed his way into your and Appa's heart. The mist of lies had somehow stayed.

Looking back now, I see the self-absorbed youngster; the chameleon-like man who easily adapted to fit any scenario; the lover who never really spoke of dreams of the future and of a family. I was head over heels in love. Which is worse: that I was blinded by a fantasy or that I was careless to the signs?

I never told you about the first time he slapped me. It wasn't even after our marriage. This was way back when we were still in college. It was at the convocation. You and Appa had come, dressed to the nines. You had been so proud of me and I couldn't have been happier. I remember being surrounded by people who loved and supported me. Arpit stood by me in a corner and waited silently, as I soaked up all the praise with a blush.

I was ecstatic. A graduation behind me and a boyfriend walking by my side, with his arm hooked around mine. We strolled down a poorly lit pathway, to the sound of shy insects and restless birds. He stopped and took my shoulders in his hands, as he stared into my eyes with an expression I had never seen before. Stupid! Stupid! Stupid! I thought that it was love or maybe even passion or desire. I truly thought that, until I felt the sting on my cheek as I fell backwards and landed on the gravel. He stomped away, leaving me there on the ground with my questions. Something was very wrong and I didn't see it.

The next day, the transformation was very dramatic. He turned into a heart-broken Romeo and pleaded in all earnestness that jealousy had forced him to lose control. After a bit of persuading, I gave in and soaked up all his attention, like a delusional teenager. I forgave him because I had somehow convinced myself that that had been the last time. It wasn't.

Flipping through the crisp pages of my wedding album brought back the whirlwind memories of my special day. I was under the impression that I had been as ecstatic as any bride. The pictures, however, screamed a different kind of distortion. My face held a shadow. Some of the photos revealed a slight cringe, while he seemed genuinely happy. Overall, my smiles were plastic and pasted on.

Slowly, it all came back to me today, ma. Appa was dying of cancer. You were excited about getting me married off and that Appa was having the chance to see me settle down.

We had been dating for five years by then. To break off the engagement would have been an affront in the face of tradition. I felt like I was powerless to change my destiny. So, I did nothing. Allowing myself to become numb, I went through the motions of a ceremony.

Eventually, it was all over. We spent a week visiting relatives and finishing up the formalities in each other's homes. Just after that, we left for our month long honeymoon to Singapore. It was a bizarre series of events. A pattern of passion and punishment emerged from our rancid relationship. At first, he would slap me around only once a week. But, as I got to know him a little better, he increased the abuse as he saw fit. At one point, I broke his favourite mug by accident

A PATTERN OF PASSION AND PUNISHMENT EMERGED FROM OUR RANCID RELATIONSHIP

and he slammed his hand against my body like I was a lump of dough. I screamed and begged for mercy, a mercy that never came.

Over the years, I was forced to learn ways in which I could work around his outbursts. I used feminine wiles, aggressive retaliations and tears to side step his assaults. It finally came down to whether or not I would live to see another day. I put all my strength into trying to change him and understand the source of his anger. But, he would not let me in and he controlled my every move.

The worst was when I was pregnant with Anant. By then, I was in too deep. He would batter me twice a week, like clockwork, and then a few times more, whenever he got drunk. You never knew he had a serious drinking problem, did you? He hid it well because everyone was under the impression that he was a very religious man and I didn't want to die. I *have given up religion. It has cost me much. How much? I would wonder where God was when my husband would get up off his knees from prayer and kick me.*

Ma, it wasn't always bad. Sometimes, I would get a glimpse of the man I had fallen in love with. He would hold me close and stroke my hair gently. I would almost forget the man he really is. I would let myself go and memorize every millisecond of that moment. When things became awful again, I would pull those memories out and savour them.

But how long can I live on memories? I tell myself that I must never let hope come alive. It hurts much worse than the blows. Hope to me, now, is to close my eyes and never open them again. Once this is over, I won't hurt anymore. I love you.

Your Daughter,

Lily

Lily's hands shook each time she swallowed a bunch of pills with water. A whole box of them went into her. She felt strangely still once the deed was done. She walked over to her bed and stretched out over it. She closed her eyes and waited. She waited to become no more.

∼∾∾◁╫▷∾∾∼

CHAPTER ONE

When Love Goes Missing

"All the most powerful emotions come from chaos, fear, anger, love-especially love. Love is chaos itself. Think about it! Love makes no sense. It shakes you up and spins you around. And then, eventually, it falls apart."

— Kirsten Miller, The Eternal Ones

*I*n the narratives I have presented to you, there is a common and very disturbing factor. The battered wives did not realize that they were not living but that they were eking out an existence, in an abusive marital relationship. That violence was a crime punishable by law, that they had the right to seek relief from such a situation, was not immediately apparent to them.

Is there such a thing as "eternal love"? Does love always have to die after the wedding day? Is there anything that can salvage a marriage that hides dying love behind a festering life-sized wound? Let us set out together on that long and painful voyage, of learning restoration in a marriage gone out of control. It will hurt and ache, and perhaps burn the soul from reopening old scars, but let us endure. Until we ultimately claim victory over abuse, a victory that can become rightfully ours.

It is every little girl's dream. Well, almost every little girl's dream, for there are exceptions. To find that fairy tale.

Most little girls dream up colorful scenarios of their wedding day and of setting up their dream home. The beautiful white dress they will wear, their exquisitely intricate hairstyle, their sparkling Cinderella slippers, the guests who will look at them with awe and admiration, and of course, the dashing groom, waiting to snatch them up onto a majestic horse and ride away towards the beginning of a new chapter in life called "happily ever after." Then, the dream transitions into a new home.

So, a little girl's play time is filled with games like "house-house," cooking on little plastic stoves, and having a fairy tale marriage with adorable, imaginary children. While she might play these games amid laughter and giggles with other little girls, she has already started picturing, with vivid details, the actual wedding day and the setting up of her dream home.

Sure enough, many little girls will have that fairy tale wedding, the prince charming, and the beautiful home. However, sadly, a few will end up being physically, mentally, and emotionally abused by their husbands. Husbands that their parents chose for them or that they fell in love with. The dream can sometimes turn into a nightmare.

These nightmarish marriages turn out to be a series of traps, into which the unsuspecting victims fall. For these women who find themselves in the said nightmare, marriage turns out to be nothing but a never-ending stream of misery, so far removed from the dreams of their childhood. These women live lives of quiet desperation, lacking the necessary courage to end their lives because they feel the need to stay alive for their children.

Knowing that they would have to endure their pain in silence and fool the world around them, they pretend to be the cherished wives of loving husbands and the happy mothers of bubbly children. Many parents, siblings, and friends are clueless about the pain that these abused women have to endure day after day, year after year. Those people who are aware of these things, often choose to stay silent and look the other way. Many of them believe the unspoken lie: that a husband has the right to discipline his wife, however he chooses. Slapping her around, being tight-fisted with money and keeping her in a constant state of fear are some of the more common tactics in use. While most women live through this kind of a life, a few go beyond the edge of desperation to finally end their misery by committing suicide. They don't see any way out of their miserable existences and prefer death instead.

Let's pause for a moment and take a look at the dreams of the other half of humankind-what do little boys dream of?

I took a look at a survey conducted by Yahoo! on the subject and the answers included were as follows: "star wars"; "becoming my favorite super hero"; "getting big and strong and saving the world"; "winning the world series"; "muscle cars and becoming a sports icon."

Not one boy mentioned wanting a great marriage or

having a great family. Then again, not a single reply revealed the makings of a potential wife-beater; you couldn't see it anywhere between the lines. It appears that everybody dreams of a "happily ever after", boys included. So, from which dark corner of creation did "wife battery" emerge? We will get to that in a later section. The only point I am trying to make here is that you will not find this text perpetuating the "men are monsters" myth. But, rest assured, these pages will not spare the abuser.

What you can expect from this book is an investigation of the definition of marital abuse, what it looks like in real life situations and how to heal from the wounds that abuse leaves behind. Do not for a moment suspect that we are going soft on our mission. Violence against women is a crime—a national, political, social, physical and spiritual crime. Men who raise their hands against their wives have no place in

THIS BOOK IS AN INVESTIGATION OF THE DEFINITION OF MARITAL ABUSE AND HOW TO HEAL FROM THE WOUNDS THAT ABUSE LEAVES BEHIND

civilized society and not for one minute are we condoning such acts. Our priority **is** the woman—to save her and to remove her from the hell she is imprisoned in. Either that, or we must come up with ways in which she can prove to the bully that he will not get away with abuse.

However, part of the agenda is to help such abusive men realize that there is hope for them as well. There is a way they can be rehabilitated from their abusive behaviors, and can live decent, respectful lives with their families. Many of them are from families where they saw their fathers beating their mothers and getting away with it. But that time has firmly passed by, and they need to understand that. Today, women are more aware of their rights and of how they can

seek protection from abuse. The number of government laws, helplines and NGOs supporting abused women are on the rise. It won't be long before a wife-beater will find himself behind bars, with his life in ruins. I believe in prayer and deliverance for these men, but sometimes redemption comes at a cost.

In the meantime, for their emotional stability, it is important for the battered wives, who have walked out of marriages and who have chosen to make new lives for themselves, to understand the factors that surrounded the making of their abusive husbands. Once it is understood that there exists bad experiences that do untold damage to a man's psyche, which in turn cause his personality to degenerate, the wife would find it easier to forgive her abusive husband and move on with her life, without constantly replaying the past. (No, it is not necessary for her to go back to him if she doesn't want to). Be that as it may, let us get back to the theme of the book by looking at three marriages that began with hope but quickly descended into disaster.

WHAT HAPPENED TO THE MAN I MARRIED?

Varda and Shalini grew up together, having attended the same kindergarten and lived in adjoining houses. They played and studied together, even when they attended different high schools, since their curriculums were similar. Both of them ended up choosing commerce in college and continued to remain best friends, who spent a lot of time in each other's company.

Enter Nikil, a classmate and good friend who asked if he could study with them. They agreed. During the course of their many study sessions together, Varda and Nikil fell in love. Shalini got married soon after graduating, and Nikil and Varda decided to follow suit by getting married, after a period of courting. Varda came from a wealthy family, while Nikil was from an average middle class family. Initially, Varda's parents opposed the marriage, but subsequently gave in. Varda and Nikil were soon married and found good jobs. From the start, Nikil felt it would be better if they used one bank account—namely his—as it would be easier to keep track of their finances, and save up for the house they hoped to buy some day. Operating from just one account made sense to Varda as well, and so she happily agreed, knowing that her own mother had also obeyed the rules that her father had laid down. Varda was eager to please her new husband, and so she went along with whatever he decided.

After a while, asking her husband for permission to spend money from their joint account became a little tedious, especially when it involved buying little things here and there. Even more frustrating was the fact that most of her requests were ignored. In addition to working a full-time job, Varda was expected to keep a clean and tidy home and cook every day. Nikil didn't share in any of the household responsibilities and, over time, started getting very critical both about Varda's housekeeping and the food she cooked. At first, his remarks seemed harmless, but soon, they became rude and insulting.

Nikil eventually started criticizing her looks and then began degrading her, by calling her fat and ugly. He wanted Varda to be available for him anytime he felt the urge to have sex. If she did not show interest or willingly participate in his sexual demands, he would accuse her of being unfaithful with other men. Getting ready for office became unbearable as Nikil would keep taunting her about the men she was going to sleep with at office. She downplayed the way she dressed, so that she would not attract unwanted attention. Even the tiniest scratch on her body earned her verbal abuse, suggesting that she had obtained the said mark by indulging in physical relations with somebody else. She found it very difficult to withstand Nikil's cruel remarks and wanted to share her problems with her parents. But as they were quite old, she held her tongue, hoping that things would eventually get better and that she'd have the marriage she had always wanted.

As the years went by, her marriage grew from bad to worse. Nikil and Varda were blessed with two lovely girls. The girls never saw much of their father and he wasn't very involved in their upbringing. Once they got a little older, he became a more hands-on father and started to dote on his girls. Varda was left out of PTA meetings and other outings. By now, Nikil had started hitting and verbally abusing Varda on a daily basis. The girls never once thought that their father was wrong but firmly believed that their mother must have done something that warranted their doting *papa*'s angry response. Nikil resisted every attempt his girls made towards building a relationship with their mother and succeeded in keeping their relationships strained.

In the seventh year of marriage, Varda met her childhood friend, Shalini. Unfortunately, whatever friendship she thought might be rekindled with Shalini was soon lost, as she found that Nikil and Shalini were growing close. Shalini was also having marital troubles and poured out all her woes to Nikil. Shalini became a permanent fixture in Varda's house and, as time passed, Shalini and Nikil became more intimate. They started going out as a couple. Varda's angry protests were met with beatings with belts, sticks, even a stool. After a particularly severe beating, Varda finally decided to go to her parents and pour her heart out to them. But, Nikil showed up and managed to convince them that he loved her but had only been upset because she was having an extramarital affair with someone in her office. The parents secretly believed him over their own daughter. They coaxed and cajoled her, and sent her back home.

Varda finally realized that she would never get any support from her family and that she was all alone in her hopeless situation.

Thereafter, not only did Varda have to watch the blatant closeness between Nikil and Shalini, she had to cook for them as well. The girls soon noticed that something was amiss in their parents' marriage but, instead of confronting their father, they told their mother that she must adjust and not do anything to aggravate the palpable tension at home. So, that is exactly what Varda did. She kept quiet and took all the emotional, financial and physical abuse that was meted out to her. She watched in silence, as another woman carved a permanent place for herself in her own home. The only attention she got from her husband was when he chose to spew horrible words at her, whenever he felt she needed to be taught a lesson. Her life's mission was to cook, clean and earn for him.

Sadly, Varda's situation is very real and hasn't changed much over the years. Though at one stage, she was so desperate that she came to see me, I soon understood that she had no intention of permanently dealing with the situation. She believed it was her *kismet* and had hoped I would provide a magic wand which would make everything okay. She was very clear that she would not take any action—she would not confront her husband anymore, since it only made him more violent. She could never leave her husband because that would affect the chances her daughters had of contracting good marriages.

The constant physical and psychological abuse has taken its toll on her. She is overweight and has a slew of health problems, which she suffers through silently. She performs her daily activities mechanically and has become completely incapable of any emotional response to the outside world. Of late, even her children have begun to mimic their father's behavior, by disrespecting her and chiding her for not retaliating. They have even told Varda, to her face, that Shalini would have made a better mother. These attitudes have seeped into her professional life, as she finds herself constantly being derided by her colleagues. It didn't take long for Varda to start believing the negative and discouraging remarks thrown at her. She sees herself as a "vegetable—alive only because I have no choice."

WHY WASN'T I WARNED IT WOULD BE LIKE THIS?

Rani was from a traditional family, which believed that if girls are not married off by the age of 17, they would land themselves in "trouble." A quiet and obedient child from the start, Rani was ready to submit to her parents' wishes for her life; she found it easy, since she had seen all her cousins doing the same.

Her parents found a groom for her and the marriage was fixed. A few days before the wedding, the groom was arrested for fraudulent activities and the wedding was quickly called off. To save face and fulfill tradition, Rani was quickly married off to another groom, Krishna, an army *jawan*, who was 15 years older than her.

Her wedding night was one of the worst nights of her entire life. As per tradition, the bride and groom retired to their room, along with generous portions of fruits, sweets, and a glass of milk. While Rani shyly waited for her groom to instruct her on what was required in the consummation process, without uttering a single word or sparing a thought about being gentle with his virgin bride, her husband quickly consummated the marriage.

Rani remembers being in agony, shell-shocked and embarrassed at the sight of her blood. Krishna proceeded to consume the sweets and fruit, and to gulp down the milk, before going to sleep. Soon, he was snoring obnoxiously. She was extremely baffled by his odd behavior but kept quiet. She wondered if all marriages were like this, as she was thoroughly naïve and uninformed. The days that followed the wedding were not much better. Her husband coerced her into having sex with him four to five times a day. To her horror, she discovered that her husband had had quite an active sexual life prior to their marriage.

As time passed, she uncovered more information about her husband's family and every discovery was worse than the one before. Krishna's mother was an abusive alcoholic. Having started drinking when he was 16, Krishna himself was a raging alcoholic by his 30s. Rani realized that her parents had unwittingly married her to an alcoholic, who was extremely abusive. She could never forget the day she discovered the extent of his bad temper. When he had gone to bed without eating his food, Rani asked him to eat and not sleep on an empty stomach, since he had consumed large quantities of alcohol. He hit her so hard that she sat back stunned. Though other family members were present when this happened, no one said a word! They continued to do whatever it is that they were doing, as though nothing had happened.

After confiding in her family about the incident and a few other similar episodes, Rani's parents made Krishna and Rani move into a rented property near their own home. Nothing changed. In fact, Krishna grew more verbally and physically abusive. He started belittling her every day, calling her a prostitute and other degrading names. He even began hurling abuse at her parents. Once when they had a small argument, Krishna bit Rani's shoulder in a fit of rage and she felt like she was being bitten by an animal. He calmly went to sleep afterwards, while Rani sobbed her heart out and decided to commit suicide. However, before she could begin to plan her suicide, she suddenly felt as if a tender hand had touched her and she felt comforted; for the first time in many months, she had a good night's rest. When she woke up the next morning, she didn't feel any pain. She realized that the touch was clearly a divine encounter of some kind.

After a few months, Krishna and Rani found that they were expecting their first child. After a caesarean, the couple was blessed with a beautiful baby boy. Instead of marveling at the birth of his son, all Krishna wanted to know was how soon they could have sexual intercourse again. Her husband's insensitivity and selfishness sent Rani into a fresh bout of depression. Once again, thoughts of suicide began to plague her.

In the midst of being a new mother and battling with depression, someone told her about the love of Jesus. Jesus soon became her lifeline. She accepted Jesus as her Savior and started attending church with her mother. She began to feel alive again and started to pick up the pieces of her life. She studied further, doing some courses, and felt excited about her life again. Her joy knew no limits when her husband got transferred to Gulmarg, Jammu and Kashmir. She decided not to join him and stayed back, using their son's education as an excuse. Krishna seemed to have no problem with that.

Her joy was short-lived, as Krishna would torture her and leave her physically and emotionally shattered every time he visited. When they went out, he would call her the foulest names in public. When she asked him why he felt the need to abuse her in front of other people, he smugly explained that she was worth nothing more. His consumption of alcohol increased as did his bad moods. Rani's life became miserable. The beatings and criticism soared. One night, while she was sleeping at her parents' house, Krishna hit her so hard that she screamed; her mother rushed into the room and saved her.

Following this, her family insisted on their going to a marriage counselor but, after a few sessions, they realized that Krishna had serious behavioral conditions that couldn't be resolved with counseling. Krishna returned to his posting and Rani was back to her life without him. After a few weeks, she learnt that he was admitted in the army hospital, diagnosed with a mental disorder. His constant drinking and rage had got Krishna into trouble at work as well. Finally, Rani summoned the courage to leave him. Krishna begged her pastor to convince her to take him back. He claimed that without her, he would die, and promised that he would quit drinking. The pastor and the church elders asked her to try to save her marriage, one last time. So, she tried; nothing changed. She knew then, in her heart, that Krishna would never change.

Finally, after deliberating over her situation, Rani decided to file for divorce. Krishna couldn't stomach the fact that she was finally leaving him and he caused more than a few drunken scenes outside her home. She was advised to join a centre for victims of abuse. After weeks of counseling, Rani filed for divorce.

More than two years, 25 court visits, and thousands of rupees later, Rani is still in the middle of divorce proceedings. She chose not to report his violent behavior to the court or to the police, which has resulted in the prolonging of her case.

No matter what happens, she has come to realize that she could never live with him. She has already begun to carve out a new life for herself and her son.

How Dare He Think I'm Going To Let Him Get Away With It?

Mini, an interior designer, moved in as my neighbor, with her son, Anirudh. I couldn't believe it when she said her son was in Standard X. She looked too young to have a son that age! She came from a wealthy family that had its roots in Kerala. We soon became good friends and she poured out her heart to me.

Her parents had arranged her marriage to Vignesh, who came from an equally wealthy background. As soon as they had gotten married, Vignesh told her to quit her job and take care of the house. Mini became a fulltime homemaker and was quite content at first. Then, Vignesh gradually started to change. His office timings became erratic and he would come home very late. He never asked her if she wanted to go out and never invited her along, when he did go out. Mini soon realized that her husband had a very nasty temper. When angry, he would shove and bang furniture and he would even throw eggs all over the place.

Mini's response was to keep silent and quickly restore order in the house, before she had to face the wrath of his fists. She knew this from experience. Vignesh began to doubt her faithfulness, so much so that, even quick trips to the shop would earn her the title "prostitute". Vignesh didn't share chores around the house but constantly belittled and insulted her. Mini was tempted to confide in her parents but held back, since she didn't want them to feel bad or worry about her. Further, she was also under the impression that all marriages were the same and that, behind locked doors, maybe even her father abused her mother—who knew?

Within a year, Mini and Vignesh were blessed with a baby boy and they named him, Anirudh. Anirudh became the center of her universe. Nothing changed regarding her husband or her marriage, and Vignesh continued to abuse her for the smallest of things. When Anirudh was just 4 years old, he could sense the tension between his parents, and every time his father raised his hand to hit his mother, Anirudh would come charging at his father in his mother's defense.

One such instance earned Anirudh a hard smack. Something snapped in Mini. Not wanting her son to share her fate, she finally decided to leave Vignesh. The first thing she did was call her parents. Thankfully, they were attending a wedding nearby and rushed to see her. She poured out all the sadness and turmoil that had been building up within her over the years. They were shocked and deeply saddened by all that their daughter had gone through. They whisked their daughter and Anirudh away to Kerala.

After a few weeks of serious thought, Mini decided to file for divorce. Vignesh said that he couldn't care less but agreed to give her the divorce, if she agreed to never seek compensation from him. Mini felt that she didn't need the compensation. All she wanted was for her life to be the way it was before Vignesh came into it. Within six months, the divorce came through.

Not wanting to waste another minute of her life, Mini started to hone her professional skills and within six months of her divorce, she started a small interior designing business. Mini's business picked up. Rohann (the person whom she rented her office space from) and she became friends. The friendship turned into a serious courtship and, just barely two months later, they tied the knot. Everything seemed so perfect for Mini. Her new husband and son got along well and her parents seemed to like Rohann. They all stayed together at her parents' house. After three months, Rohann had to shift to another office, which was quite far from their residence. Mini thought it was best that she leave Anirudh with her parents, while she set up her new home.

Things seemed fine at first but Rohann's personality seemed to change rapidly. Mini could not believe it was happening again; the man she married had begun to morph into a beast. Was it something in her that made the men change and become violent? Rohann started abusing her and calling her names. He forbade her to talk to her parents and son in his absence, and monitored every single call she made or received. Mini was not allowed to interact with anyone and, if he caught her doing it, he degraded her and called her the foulest of names.

His mood swings were what puzzled Mini the most. One minute, he would hold her in his arms and say that she was the most beautiful woman in the world, and the next minute, he would physically and verbally abuse her, saying that she looked like the backend of a bus. This began to happen on a daily basis. It even reached a stage where Rohann would hit Mini in his sleep, saying that she was disturbing him. Even in that subconscious state, he struck out at her. Worse, he never expressed the slightest remorse over his actions.

Rohann became a sex addict and pressured her to have sex with him many times in a single day. Whether she was sleeping, cooking or doing housework, whenever the urge to have sex presented itself to him, he felt it was her duty to satisfy him. Mini felt like an animal. She became increasingly revolted by the way he treated her in bed. The slightest delay in satisfying him would result in her getting a severe beating. One day, she just caved in and had a nervous breakdown.

Her parents and Anirudh came to see her and, after finding her in a dazed and agitated state, they had her admitted in a hospital. Mini was diagnosed with chronic depression, and it took more than six months of counseling and medication for her to return to normal. Her old fearful and anxious personality seemed to be replaced by a more assertive and bold version. She regained control of her life and the first thing she did was leave Rohann. She approached one of the best marital lawyers she could find and worked her way out of the mess she was in. Mini filed a case of torture and harassment and applied for divorce, due to domestic violence. She took all her medical reports and sought a staggering amount of compensation. The court didn't make it easy for her and after a hard legal battle, finally emerged victorious. Wanting to begin a new journey for herself and Anirudh, she had moved to a new city and started life in a new apartment. For her, money had never been a problem.

I was happy to have Mini as my neighbor. At the time, her case had not been closed yet, and she was still fighting it out in court, so that she got every rupee that she felt was owed to her. She didn't mind if she lost all her money in fighting her case but she refused to leave Rohann in peace till he paid up. Mini wasn't just keen on teaching Rohann a lesson. She wanted her story to be a wakeup call for all those men who abused their wives; they must know that women were not going to simply look the other way or run away, but they were going to make abusive men pay! Mini was one of the bold ones who told me that I could use their real names in this book.

But naturally, I changed all the identities; I believe it is the wise thing to do.

What Is The Irony In All Three Situations?

Varda, Rani, and Mini: three young women who didn't receive any love from their spouses. For them, marriage was a place of constant turmoil, fear, abuse, and stress. It was never the romantic and safe relationship that they had dreamt of.

In the narratives I have presented to you, there is a common and very disturbing factor. The battered wives did not realize that they were not living but that they were eking out an existence, in an abusive marital relationship. That violence was a crime punishable by law, that they had a right to seek relief from such a situation, was not immediately apparent to them. Here are some of the excerpts from their remarks:

> "I thought he just had a bad temper...He hit me but he loved me too..."

> "I felt maybe all husbands behave like this with their wives, especially Indian men..."

> "I don't know when and how it started and why I put up with it. I certainly did not think it was abuse at that time. I simply put it down to my bad luck, and did not think of it as abuse..."

Good grief! If that thought process is what you (beloved reader) are also struggling with, then it is absolutely essential that you find out exactly what constitutes abuse in a marriage, before we go any further.

CHAPTER TWO

Abuse: Towards a Definition

"All marriages are sacred, but not all are safe."

— Rob Jackson

*I*n front of others, my husband treats me like a queen—he opens doors for me, praises my beauty, boasts about my cooking, and tells everyone how lucky he was to get me. On the other hand, when we are alone at home, he ignores me completely, and most of the time locks himself in our bedroom. When I ask him why he's acting like this, he answers irritably in monosyllables or asks me to "Shut up." At times, he even slaps me. His mood swings are driving me mad and I don't know how much longer I can put up with this. Am I being abused?

There is no marriage that is devoid of conflict. All couples have their share of marital problems and it would be difficult to find a couple who has not had a serious argument or where one of the two has not threatened to leave the other. But, abuse and violence within a relationship should never be confused with everyday conflicts. The hallmark of an abusive relationship is a systematic pattern of control through violence.

Which of the following, in your opinion, constitutes abuse?

AN ABUSIVE RELATIONSHIP IS A SYSTEMATIC PATTERN OF CONTROL THROUGH VIOLENCE

- A slap or two?
- Being shoved around roughly?
- Being subjected to foul language?
- Being forced to have sex against one's will?
- Humiliation or put-downs in front of other people?
- No freedom of any kind and being constantly deprived of finances?
- Not being allowed to have a social life outside the home?
- Being subjected to frequent violent outbreaks?

With the many questions that plague women and the endless stream of bad advice that is often given to them by their communities, there is a dire need for answers. This chapter is an investigation into the essence of what abuse is, and the various forms in which it appears.

Her marriage was full of apologies, false promises and crocodile tears. The relationship was a decade-old. Every day started with fresh hope: that the new day would be different and that the abuse would finally become a thing of the past. But, every now and then, she would be covered with bruises on her arms or back. Every time he saw his handiwork, he would break down and promise to never raise his hand against her again.

She was to blame for the beatings she received, she would say to herself. If only she knew how to talk, if only she knew how to dress, if only her cooking skills were not so sub-standard...

> SHE WAS ALIVE ONLY IN A PURELY BIOLOGICAL SENSE, A MERE VEGETABLE EXISTING BECAUSE HER BODY WAS THERE

The amazing part of this situation was that he could lay the blame at her door so convincingly, that soon she believed it was her fault that her husband was always angry with her. If he didn't beat her, how else would she learn the right way to behave? The truth was that she was in love with a volatile man, who was trying to destroy her— her health, her self-esteem, her values and her very reason to live—and whose only mission seemed to be to inflict pain on his wife.

The situation only grew worse over time, till he managed to completely destroy her. Till she was alive only in a purely biological sense, a mere vegetable existing because her body was there. Her mind, heart and emotions had shut down a long time ago.

Poor woman! Little did she know that she was trapped in the giant spiderweb of an abusive relationship. This kind of abuse generally follows a three-stage cycle:

1. *Tension Building Stage:* During this phase the abusive partner stockpiles every little grievance and every disappointment he has experienced. By twisting her words, he tries to portray them her fault. The victim develops an awful fear as she feels that she can't do

anything right and that she may trigger her partner's angry outbursts. This stage can last from a few hours to a few months. It is scary, waiting and wondering what he will do and when his anger will break out.

2. ***The Battering Stage:*** During this stage, often over a trivial issue, the abuser bursts out with screaming, hurtful and frightening aggression, dominating and controlling his partner through a number of violent and abusive incidents.

3. ***The Honeymoon Stage:*** After the abusive phase, most of the abusers act ashamed, expressing regret that the violence happened and promising that it will never recur. He might take her to the doctor if she requires medical assistance (makes sure that a lie is told to explain the bruises), and might threaten self-harm or suicide if the victim plans to leave him. However, not all abusive relationships have this phase.

This cycle puts pressure on the victim to give the abuser yet another chance, even though she has been badly abused. Such an abusive man seems to be a nice gentleman whose gentleness is hidden under his abusiveness; though he hits at times, he sounds wounded later, yearning for love. Hope springs eternal in the woman's heart, and she believes with all her heart that he will change, even though the abuser had made this promise a hundred times before and failed to keep it. She believes that he will change. Sometimes even relatives and friends pressurize her to give him a chance again, because of his gentlemanly behavior. Typically, after a brief respite, the beast inside that hurt child takes over; he abuses her again, and the cycle repeats itself.

Sadly the outside world sees only the tip of the iceberg. Thus, when you examine the subject of abuse, it looks very ambiguous and hopelessly confusing. Many couples fail to realize that some relationships can be worked out, while some cannot.

Many who have come to me for help feel as if they have fallen into an abandoned well, with no way to climb out and no one to hear their pleas. My heart aches for them as I write this.

It is of vital importance to define abuse. When people think of abuse, they usually visualize physical acts of violence. In reality, abuse within a relationship can take on different forms. It may be emotional, mental, financial or verbal, and this may eventually escalate to physical abuse.

To get a very clear and objective understanding of what constitutes abuse, let us together examine the true accounts of a few women. They have expressed their doubts and want to know whether they are in a situation of abuse. Situations vary for different couples. With the help of the insight that has helped me, you will be able to judge what exactly constitutes abuse in a marriage.

VERBAL ABUSE

Vina: I have been married for eight years now. From day one, my husband has spoken to me using extremely derogatory terms and foul language. Sometimes, he does this even in front of the children or the maid servant. When I tell him not to speak in this manner to me, he threatens me. Is this abuse?

Yes. Constantly being subjected to abusive language, whether while alone or in the presence of others, is the denigration of your status as wife and mother. Being repeatedly undermined in this manner, gradually erodes your confidence and self-esteem and, subsequently, affects the way your children perceive and respect you. You have to address this issue quite seriously.

Sarla: The comments started out as "harmless jokes" made in good humor. However today, after five years of marriage, his constant remarks— about my cooking being terrible, about my having no dress sense, his rude remarks that I am shaped like a tent or that I laugh too loud, etc— are not funny anymore. Should I consider this as abuse? I must honestly say that my husband does not use foul language.

Let me ask you if you have ever sat down with your husband and told him how you feel about his demeaning remarks? If you have and he has ignored your protests, continuing with the mockery, it borders on verbal abuse. If not firmly curtailed, it could lead to unhappier situations. You can have a serious discussion with him, making sure you tell him how you feel. You can also find out whether he has any constructive suggestion which you might be able to agree together.

Vinotha: I have been fortunate in securing a good position in my company. Now I earn much more than my husband. However, ever since I acquired this position, he has been consumed with doubt and jealousy. This has manifested in various ways, like insulting me or embarrassing me in front of my friends and family. If I happen to come late from work, he accuses me of sleeping around. In fact, he once asked me who my new flame was in front our 16-year-old son! He listens in whenever I get a phone call, eavesdropping even if it is a conversation with my mom or my brothers. He has become very controlling, calls me terrible names and keeps an account of every rupee I spend. I do not want to oppose him, as things turn very ugly and it takes weeks to get back to normal. Even then, it is only when I apologize, which I do just to reduce the tension in the house. I am sick of this kind of maligning of my character and of all his insinuations. I am under constant stress. What should I do?

Your situation is one of emotional and psychological abuse. If your husband has major issues with you earning more than he does, try to explain to him the importance of having such an income. After all, he stands to benefit as well! Gently but firmly tell him that you will not tolerate being put down in this manner. It will be good for all concerned, especially your son, whose character is being formed based on the models he sees before him. You have to lay down proper boundaries, and insist on their not being crossed. Creating healthy boundaries is empowering, as these boundaries protect your sense of self-esteem and your ability to live out your full potential.

MENTAL ABUSE OR MIND GAMES

Sarah: My husband declares that he loves me very much and trusts me; at the same time, he insists on regularly checking my emails and SMSs. If I go out for a wedding or with my friends, or if I am out of station, he calls me up many times. I get so rattled that I hardly have time to relate to anyone else. It's like he is keeping a track of me. Whenever he is unable to reach me, he calls my friends. I feel I am under observation every minute I am away from him. Is this the normal way in which all husbands behave or am I just overreacting?

My dear Sarah, certainly not. Your privacy is being invaded, and it is very natural for you to feel disgruntled. This is a typical mind game that many men play—your husband puts on a front of pretending to love and trust you, but he is being eaten up by needless suspicion. There seems to be a "control freak" in him. A lot of it depends on the rules the two of you have set up for your marriage. Since he reads your emails and keeps constant tabs on you, have you asked him if he would be comfortable with you monitoring his every move or reading all his mails? Though his behavior can be seen as deplorable, it cannot be strictly categorized as abusive behavior yet. But, in the long run, this behavior can increase and end up in abuse.

Poornima: Ours was a love marriage. We come from different religious backgrounds — my husband is Muslim and I am Hindu. When we married, he promised that he would never force me to follow his religious ways, or stop me from performing my daily puja and going to the temple. He also assured me that he would make our children adhere to both religions. Now, our children are eleven and nine, and he is using deceptive ways to turn them against me and my religion. The other day my daughter said to me, "No Amma, I am not coming to the temple anymore." When she told me some of the things my husband has said to the two children about my religion, I realized that he is trying to brainwash them into following only his religion. When I confront him, he just smiles. How should I deal with this combustible situation?

Poornima, inter-religious marriages often have serious repercussions. In the glow of love, many a rash promise is made. Once you enter into the reality of marriage and face the awesome responsibility of bringing up your children, then comes the day of reckoning. That is when the conflict between the perspectives you have been brought up with and the deep individual convictions you have, comes to the forefront. It is a delicate situation and you will need to tread very carefully as "God" would hate to be the cause of a rift between you. Instead of manipulating and resorting to subtle mind games, wisdom would lie in sitting at the table as a family and sensitively discussing the issue. The situation has not yet gotten out of hand, nor has abuse come into it. If you are careful, it won't. Speak in love to your husband and tell him to keep the children's best interests in mind. Surely, some compromise can be worked out.

Seema: In front of others, my husband treats me like a queen—he opens doors for me, praises my beauty, boasts about my cooking, and tells everyone how lucky he was to get me. On the other hand, when we are alone at home, he ignores me completely and, most of the time, locks himself in our bedroom. When I ask him why he acts like this, he answers irritably in monosyllables or asks me to "Shut up." At times, he even slaps me. His mood swings are driving me mad and I don't know how much longer I can put up with this. Am I being abused?

Seema, you may not be aware of it but this is one of the most subtle forms of abuse. Psychologists refer to this kind of behavior as the "Dr. Jekyll and Mr. Hyde Syndrome." This type of personality fluctuates from being extremely kind and considerate to being extremely vicious or withdrawn within minutes. The constant hot-and-cold-water type of treatment drives the recipient crazy. Some might not even realize that they are being abused because good behavior follows the bad behavior almost instantaneously. Living with this type of a person becomes an emotional roller coaster ride, as you are living with someone who has two vastly different sides. It is like having a time bomb in your bag that is ready to explode at any time. Your husband needs treatment and you have to be aware that you are in a very difficult situation, which needs the intervention of God and others who will handle the matter wisely.

SEXUAL ABUSE

Lina: I realize I am in a terrible situation, as far as my marriage is concerned. Our normal arguments are often accompanied by physical violence. The arguments may be over very minor issues, but that is enough to send my husband into a fit of rage. He forces me to have intimate relations with him and participate in revolting sexual activities, at times even when I am not interested or when I am in deep sleep. He berates me and accuses me of being frigid, and insists on touching me when I do not want to be touched. He calls me a whore and a slut, and physically attacks other parts of my body. Is this domestic violence or do all wives submit to this kind of behavior from their husbands?

Dear Lina, this is definitely domestic violence and you are being subjected to physical, emotional and sexual abuse. Such violence stems from men wanting to prove their power, contrary to the belief that they are driven by lust.

In fact, this is marital rape, which is largely overlooked by everyone. In our culture, only a few would correctly call nonconsensual sexual relations within a marriage as rape. Many do not take it seriously, nor do they treat it as a crime. Instead they merely condone it by saying that this is the way men have been for centuries. Historically, supporters of marital rape exemption have justified its continuation, on the basis of three legal points:

ALL RAPE DEHUMANIZES A PERSON AND YOUR HUSBAND DOES THIS TO ACHIEVE A SENSE OF POWER AND CONTROL

1. ***The Contract Theory,*** which suggests that a wife has contractually given a husband irrevocable consent to intercourse.

2. ***The Woman as Property Theory,*** which implies that a husband owns his wife, like he owns any other property and, therefore, cannot "take" what is already his.

3. ***The Marital Unity Theory,*** where the husband and wife merge upon marriage into one person, and the one person is the husband, thereby relegating marital rape to a legal non sequitur.

But, all rape dehumanizes a person and your husband does this to achieve a sense of power and control. If he continues this behavior, you might have to involve your relatives and seek their help to put a stop to it. If he still persists in abusing you, you might have to inform the police.

PHYSICAL ABUSE AND VIOLENCE

Anand: I often hear about wife abuse, but can men be abused in marriages? I have been married for the past three years, and we have a two-year-old daughter. The first six months of our marriage were really good, but then my wife started feeling that I did not love her or find her attractive. She would bring it up all the time, even when I came home tired from work. In the beginning, I tried to reassure her but, after a while, I got fed up. And two months ago, she became increasingly intolerant. If I did not come home at the time she expected me to or at the time I had said I would, she would blow a fuse. My "late" comings were followed by heated arguments, and she would throw plates and things at me screaming that we should get divorced. I hoped she would change. But, a week ago, she blew her fuse again, and this time she broke everything within her reach—photo frames, lamps, vases, etc. She was screaming like a mad woman, and then she went to the extent of smashing my laptop and tearing up my shirts. I had enough. I left the house. I love my wife very much, but I cannot put up with her erratic behavior. I even fear for my daughter's life. She is begging me to come back, promising me that she would get help but I am skeptical. Is this not violence in a marriage and does this not prove that it is not always the husband that is to be blamed for abuse in a marriage?

Yes, you are right, young man! It is not always the husband who is abusive in a marriage. Your wife seems to have an abusive nature as she is breaking only your items. But before deciding to move out, why don't you find out if she is struggling with any other issues, like loneliness or insecurity. Your wife needs counseling, and if she has agreed to get help, then you should support and encourage her, reassuring her of your love. Maybe she needs to be taught how to control emotions. Apart from individual counseling, your wife and you should go for marital counseling. It's not just your marriage at stake here, but also the future of your two-year-old daughter, who is now caught in the crossfire. There are anger management groups that can help her keep her anger in check. A three to six-month separation would be good at this stage, to allow her to work on her issues.

Manasi: My husband has such a violent temper; he slaps and pushes me around all the time. If his food gets a little cold, I get a slap; if I come a little late, I get a shout and a slap. The few times I've summoned the courage to defend myself, he has beaten me so badly that I couldn't get out of bed for days. I am so weary of this. When I confided in my mother-in-law, she said it was all a part of married life and that I should not provoke my husband but just stay silent. Is this abuse or is it really okay for husbands to do this?

You are being subjected to physical abuse and your husband uses his anger and rage to overpower and control you. If he's not confronted and stopped, he might cause grave injury to your person. See if you can get some family member to intervene or get him to go for a Battering Intervention and Prevention Program. If he refuses, then think about getting a restraining order and living separately for some time, until he changes his behavior. If he continues with the violence, then you have no other option but to involve the law. Section 498-A of the Indian Penal Code has a provision that prohibits cruelty towards the wife causing injury to life, limb, or health of the woman. Legal action can be taken against your husband if he doesn't mend his ways.

Kavya: This is to find out if there is a difference between marital conflict and abuse. I've heard of many couples having a marital conflict. Even in our marriage, my husband and I get into very passionate and angry arguments. Sometimes, he pushes me around in anger. I have also hit him, in the heat of the moment. I have been provoked beyond endurance and punched him too, but my punches don't cause any damage compared to his slaps and punches, which leave grievous marks. Is this marital conflict or abuse? I would really like a concise definition of what constitutes violence in a marriage. Can we go for counseling to solve the issue?

Kavya, every marriage experiences a certain amount of conflict. There may be strong arguments and bitter fights as each one fights to keep one's identity and to be in control. However, physical abuse is very different; it is a one-sided, unhealthy control. There might be times of passion, love and care in between bouts of violence, but it all usually boils down to gaining control over the other person. It can result in isolating you from friends and relatives; it can be a fight for sexual and financial control. Mad jealousies, name calling, false accusations and frequent guilt trips are part of an abusive marriage. The abuser may demand complete attention and may seek to dictate every action of his victim. Intimidation and threats become a daily affair. When the abuser reaches this stage of rage, only intervention from other family members, social organizations, or the police can stop the abuse. However, marital conflict gets resolved in time, when proper counseling is given and sound communication methods are taught in a friendly and non-judgmental atmosphere. Judging from the situation you describe, you and your husband need to work with a marriage counselor and concentrate on improving your communication skills.

EMOTIONAL ABUSE

Malika: I live with my husband and in-laws. After the first few months of marriage, my husband and my in-laws started harassing me. They constantly complained about my cooking and cleaning, and the way I dressed. They made derogatory remarks about my parents. When I protested a few times, my husband asked me to shut up and not disrespect his parents. My husband and I have been unable to have a child even after years of marriage, and my in-laws keep insisting that it is my fault and that they should never have agreed to this marriage proposal. I have been feeling very depressed off late and have not been sleeping or eating well. Am I being abused?

Malika, it certainly sounds like you are facing emotional/ psychological abuse. While physical abuse is more direct and obvious, emotional or psychological abuse is far more subtle. The abuser often resorts to playing mind games; he does so by passing critical remarks, insulting and degrading the victim, and demoralizing and attacking the victim's self-esteem and self-worth, to such an extent that the victim feels useless and lives in a constant state of rejection and hopelessness. Your husband and in-laws are trying to control you and demean you using every chance they get. If that doesn't work, they will insult you in all kinds of ways to provoke a response from you, in this case talking ill about your family. If you are unable to conceive, you may both have to see a doctor. Today, stress is a major factor that prevents many couples from having children. Environmental causes are also cited. Your husband and you must sit down and have a talk. If you allow your in-laws to negatively interfere, your marriage is doomed to fail. If you have to live with his parents, set down firm boundaries and make sure everyone adheres to it.

Mala: My husband is smarter, more educated and comes from a far better financial background than I do. I am mild and not very smart. I cannot really figure out if I am in an abusive relationship, and always wonder whether I am the one who ignites the trouble. My husband often gets provoked fast and shouts at me, but later calls himself a victim of circumstances. After every fight, my husband tells his friends that I provoked him to anger. This makes me feel guilty and I blame myself for igniting his anger. He makes sure to declare to all that if I had behaved more seemingly in the situation, then he would not have had to lose his temper. Am I the abuser or am I in an abusive situation?

Mala, there is a big difference between your husband having a bad day and your husband constantly blaming you for everything that goes wrong in his life. It sounds like you are being emotionally abused. It's not good for a marriage when either husband or wife start discussing their problems with friends. Having a few friends that mentor and genuinely listen and help you is okay, but your husband and you need to be in agreement about who these friends are. While people bring different gifts and skills into a marriage, they bring different shortcomings as well. You both need to appreciate and admire each other's gifts and skills, and be patient and tolerate the shortcomings as well.

Many wives tolerate this kind of silent emotional abuse for years, not knowing that internalizing the hurt, stress, and anxiety will cause them to get sick, hurt themselves, and generally miss living life to its fullest potential.

ECONOMIC ABUSE

Priya: I feel like I am in a crippling situation in my marriage. I have to give an account for every paise, and I mean for every paise, that I spend. I am not employed outside of home. My husband made me give up my job after our marriage. Sometimes, if I cannot account for what I've spent, my husband gets very angry and belittles me. He punishes me by not giving me sufficient money the next month or making me beg for the money. I feel so trapped, with no money for my basic needs or even to run the house. I have to stick on because I have nowhere else to go and fear losing the only support system I have. Am I facing abuse of any kind?

Yes, Priya, you are in an abusive relationship. You haven't mentioned whether you have children but, even if there are no children, every marriage is worth saving. The fact that you are not financially productive gives your husband an edge over you. Can you think of some job that you can do from home, so that you don't have to be so dependent on your husband? Your husband needs to understand that you need money to run the house and that an itemized bill every month might not be possible. Put your foot down and speak to him about the situation. You can be firm without being offensive.

Bina: My husband insisted that I transfer my entire salary into his account every month. I suggested a joint account so that we could both access the money when the need arose, but he said his idea was better. For the first few months, everything seemed to be going well, as he gave me sufficient money to run the house and for some shopping. But, now he gives me a pittance and refuses to allow me to touch my own salary. We've had heated arguments and the few months that I refused to transfer my salary into his account; he has gotten very violent with me. Is this fair?

No, Bina, it is not. Your husband wants to have complete control over your finances. Finances are usually one of the top three stress areas in a marriage. Many marriages disintegrate when finances are in disarray. Your husband withholding your money from you will lead to feelings of bitterness and anger towards him. You both will need to discuss this issue in detail and find some solution that will result in both of you being happy. There is no need for you to transfer your salary into his account. It is a foolish move and can leave you high and dry in case of an emergency. I know of a friend who was in a similar situation. She firmly refused and after the initial flare ups, he did not make that demand anymore. You need to learn to stand up for your rights while ensuring your safety.

Dear Reader, I have faced many questions (such as the above) from different men and women whom I have met in my life's journey. I have not been able to reply to all the questions that have come my way. But, I believe that the above questions and answers address a good cross-section of the various facets of abuse in marriage. To outline the characteristic behavioral traits in an abuser, based on what the victims have shared with me, here are some facts worth knowing: Some men are like cobras, with violent outbursts. Some hit from behind, when the victim least expects it. A few destroy the wife's self-worth and status by saying derogatory things about her. Many are narcissists who believe that everyone else exists solely for their pleasure and service. Some are insanely possessive about their wives and believe that every man who looks at her is lusting for her. But the most surprising and shocking part in many of these abusive relationships is that the victims are bonded emotionally in an intense manner to their violent abusers, refusing to leave them or to press charges against them. This is referred to trauma bonding or Stockholm syndrome, after a bank robbery in Stockholm, Sweden, where the hostages became emotionally bonded to their captors, and one of them even later got engaged to one of the criminals. In such situations, we stand helpless, wondering—is there any way to protect these women from their abusers? Can these abusers ever change?

CAN ANY OF THESE VIOLENT HUSBANDS EVER CHANGE?

I posed this question to Lundy Bancroft, a consultant on domestic abuse and child maltreatment and the author of "Why Does He Do That: Inside the Minds of Angry and Controlling Men" and his response was—"I don't believe a woman should be encouraged to try to work out her relationship with an abuser, because I find improvement unheard of in the absence of criminal prosecution combined with specialized batterer intervention counseling."

If it is so difficult to change an abuser. Can a victim be taught to draw boundaries to protect herself? Is it all about drawing boundaries? A boundary is a psychological dividing line that sets the distance others are allowed to approach by telling "this is where you end" or "you are crossing the line" when someone encroaches our personal space. A boundary exists for protection, as it marks the limit between acceptable behavior and behavior that causes physical or emotional harm. Clear boundaries can help to prevent us from controlling or manipulating others and also to protect and defend ourselves from those who want to control us. Many victims of abuse find it difficult to set boundaries, as they may believe that setting a boundary is rude, or they may lack the ability to set boundaries because their boundaries were blurred or violated during their childhood. If the abuse is because of a lack of boundaries, then the problem can be remedied. The victim can be taught to establish healthy boundaries and also to defend the boundaries. For example, "if you raise your hands against me next time, I will inform the neighbor," and so on. If you are planning to establish boundaries, you should also know that most probably the abuser is likely to step over the boundary line. And when you try to carry out, firmly, exactly what you said you would do, two things can then happen. The first is that the abuser might grow more violent and he may even try to damage you because you are not allowing him to control you in the way he wants to. It helps to have both support and an 'emergency' plan for what you can do in case of such a negative response. But the second, more constructive outcome, is that you simply follow through with your basic plan; and, over time, the abuser's influence will decrease, and you will gain control.

Batterers can change, if they are confronted and made accountable in the right way and over a long period—for example, through behavior modification therapies. What the abuser has become is a result of what he has acquired from situations and circumstances around him; what is learned can be unlearned! Nobody is born an abuser. Miracles are possible for those who believe and a miracle can take place through divine intervention, and through the intervention of empathetic fellow human beings who care enough for those in similar situations.

Dearest one, if you don't do something about it soon, you are putting your children in the same volatile situation. Breaking the self-demeaning lifestyle will call for immense courage and will power, but it has to be done. Otherwise, you will become an abettor (see next chapter) of the vicious cycle of abuse.

CHAPTER THREE
The Legacy of Abuse

"Thou shalt not be a victim, thou shalt not be a perpetrator, but, above all, thou shalt not be a bystander."
— *Yehuda Bauer*

As abuse is a subconscious learning from childhood, it can definitely be unlearned. One needs to recognize it and make a conscious effort to break it. This vicious cycle keeps getting transferrzed from one generation to another, and it won't stop until one decides to break free.

You'd think that after witnessing years and years of their mothers being abused, that little boys would grow up to become defenders of the helpless and little girls would grow up strong enough to fight for themselves? Wrong. These little boys and girls grow up so scarred and confused, they become like their abusive/abused parents.

The sound of a male voice exploding in angry abusive language cut through the stillness of the night. One could hear vicious slaps and the soft cries of a woman break into the quiet of the neighborhood.

Note the responses from the neighbors. In the apartment closest to the house from which the sounds emerged, two people spoke in hushed tones:

"If he goes on like that, he will kill her."

"Yes, I feel the same way but what can we do? We cannot interfere in someone else's personal matters."

"There must be something we can do. Can we not complain or at least make a phone call to the police?"

"That will spoil relationships in society. We want to live in peace and not have stress and strife with neighbors."

The other neighbors simply sighed and shut their windows quietly. In one of the rooms within that house, a weeping five-year-old boy tried to shut out the sounds of the slaps and his mother's sobs, by pressing his hands over his ears. He crumpled back into the foetal position, as if he wished to return to the security of his mother's womb.

This is an excerpt from a real life story, being re-constructed and re-enacted by *Crime Patrol*, an Indian TV serial with enviable TRPs that has been the inspiration behind many other shows in the same genre. This show had horror film enthusiasts hooked. After watching an episode from this show on a crime that actually took place in Bangalore, the details of which I am familiar with, I can say on record that the episodes are re-constructed and re-enacted with total accuracy sans exaggeration.

However, it was not with interest but deep concern that I sat through the above-mentioned episode of a man who inflicted violence on his household daily. The result of the violence is portrayed in several moving scenes:

The child becomes withdrawn and quiet, and loses all sense of the joy of being a child. Once, when his maternal grandfather tries to play a chhuk-chhuk-gadi (train-train) game with him, the boy suddenly says,

"Nanaji, may I ask you a question?"

"Sure beta, what is it?"

"Do you ever beat naniji?"

The grandfather envelopes the child in a tight hug and they both weep.

During one visit to her parents' home, the abused wife begs her mother to let her return to her parental home. She says her husband becomes enraged with every single thing that she does and that she cannot take it anymore. Her mother, however, talks her out of it by saying: "Beti, if you come home, it will become a disgrace for you and for us. Look at the bright side of your situation—at least he does not come home drunk or womanize. Remember, every marriage has some problem or the other; try to bear with it."

The young boy becomes a recluse at school and keeps away from all the other children. He cannot concentrate in class, and during recess, he sits with his tiffin box in a corner, barely touching his food. Noticing his increasing isolation, the teacher speaks to the principal, who sends for the child's mother. When the woman comes for the meeting, she has a suspicious big black mark on one side of her face. When the principal enquires about the mark, the abused wife tries to pass it off as a mosquito bite. She insists that there is nothing amiss at home that could have caused her son to become a recluse. "He has always been a shy and reserved child," she says.

The principal and the teacher know that the mother is holding something back, but they are at a loss as to how to get her to confide in them, and so are forced to let it go at that.

Later, during an English lesson, the teacher asks the students to write an essay titled, "My Family." Something within the young boy snaps, and he writes the true story of what happens daily within his home: of how his father beats his mother and how he feels bad because he cannot do anything to save his mother. The teacher and the principal are shocked; on questioning him, the boy admits fearfully that what he had written is true. The principal sends for both parents. The father sits absolutely still and silent as the principal questions him and asks if what the boy had written in the essay is true. On receiving no response, the principal has to let the matter go with a warning.

There is hell to pay at home that night. First, the man beats up his wife, like never before, telling her that she is the one who must have filled the child's head with nonsense. The boy, for the first time, runs to his mother's rescue, shouting that his mother had done nothing, that he is the one who wrote the essay on his own. On hearing that, the father begins to rain blows on the frail young child. Something shifts inside the mother, as she grabs her little boy, runs from the house and taps on the neighbor's door. The neighbors willingly take her in. The lady tells the wife to leave the husband, but the wife says, "Where would I go? I have no money, and I have no skills." The neighbor warns, "If this goes on, the cycle of abuse will continue; one day, either your son will *become a wife-beater himself or else he will live like a victim, filled with fear and anxiety all the time." The very thought drives her to take action against her husband. She files a police complaint of Domestic Abuse.*

After an investigation is conducted and proof is received, the man is taken into police custody. The wife and child move in with her parents. The wife develops a skill that will support both herself and her son, and the child begins to smile again and seems happy. The husband goes for counseling and seems to have changed his ways. He begs his wife to take him back. She declares that she never wants to see his face again.

THE FRIGHTENING REALITY

Studies show that over three million children witness violence in their homes each year and a child's exposure to the father abusing the mother is the strongest risk factor for transmitting violent behavior from one generation to the next. Thus, we can see in quantifiable terms, the importance of the topic at hand and the urgent need to find ways to redeem children who are from abusive homes.

A survey of 6,000 American families found that 50 percent of men who assault their wives, also abuse their children [2]. More recent estimates put the figure at 50- 70%.

In families where the mother is assaulted by the father, daughters are at risk of sexual abuse 6.51 times greater than girls in non-abusive families [3]. Male children who witness the abuse of mothers by fathers are more likely to become men who batter in adulthood than those male children from homes free of violence [4].

In a 36-month study of 146 children, ages 11-17, who came from homes where there was domestic violence, all sons over the age of 14 attempted to protect their mothers from attacks. Some 62% were injured in the process [5], [6].

Research also indicates that children exposed to family violence are more likely to develop social, emotional, psychological and behavioral problems than those who are not, because of the trauma they experience [7]. They tend to show more anxiety, low self-esteem, depression and anger. These disturbances affect their development and can cause adverse effects that become evident in adulthood. The world of an abused child is frightening and unpredictable. Due to the catastrophic experiences, they become dysfunctional, as fear and helplessness flood their consciousness. They develop serious trust issues, as their parents repeatedly betray their trust. Children from abusive homes are either socially withdrawn, or they show outward signs of intense rage. Some of the behavioral signs they commonly exhibit are restlessness, anger, rage, resentment, manipulative tendencies, early sexual activity, cruelty to animals, self-neglect, etc.

CHILDREN EXPOSED TO DOMESTIC VIOLENCE ARE LIKELY TO GROW UP THINKING THAT VIOLENCE IS AN ACCEPTABLE PART OF INTIMATE RELATIONSHIPS

At an early age, these children realize the importance of power and control and do everything to ensure that they are in positions of control and domination. Children who are unable to express their anger and frustration internalize their feelings and manifest these emotions through sleeping disorders, nervousness, anxiety, panic attacks, tiredness, sickness, bedwetting and nightmares.

Further, children from violent homes find themselves unable to form lasting bonds with their peers and struggle to have normal friendships. The relationships that they have with their parents are disconnected at best. Many researchers say that there is a tendency in a young abuser's mind to abuse his victim in a way that replicates his own experiences of abuse. They become violent as a means of subconsciously dealing with the trauma.

WHAT IS IMPLIED BY THE PHRASE "VICIOUS CYCLE OF ABUSE"?

The vicious cycle, or the intergenerational cycle of abuse, is the abuse that is passed from one close relative to another in a familial setting. For e.g. from a parent to a child, or from an elder sibling to a younger one. Children exposed to domestic violence are likely to develop issues in all of their relationships because they grow up thinking that violence is an acceptable part of intimate relationships. They grow up to become either the victim or the abuser. There have been many surveys that have studied this vicious cycle in India. It has been estimated that one-third of those who were abused as children will abuse their offspring. Violent patterns of spousal relationships usually are passed on to the children, beginning an intergenerational cycle that can perpetuate itself indefinitely [8]. These children who have witnessed their parents abusing one another graduate into turbulent relationships, within which they are either violent or experience violence. In a typical patriarchal context, this cycle of abuse can be explained in three stages:

1. The Abusive Stage

When the husband is the abuser and the wife the victim, abuse becomes a part of the marital relationship almost immediately. In the abusive stage, the husband may abuse both his wife and children, or only his wife. The children may be victims or witnesses to the abuse. Such an abused child is very likely to develop mental, physical and social behavioral problems and can act in three ways:

a.   The child is not bothered about the abuse and tries to side with the more powerful abuser.

b.   The child develops manipulative techniques to escape the abuse.

c.   The child develops a protective nature and rushes to protect one's mother.

The abuse weighs on the child and leads to one's becoming withdrawn from community of any kind. As the parent-child relationship provides a basic template for future relationships, abused children automatically drift into hostile, hurtful and abusive relationships.

2. The Reinforcement Stage

When a child watches the mother being abused or experiences abuse, there comes a time when the reactions of the people around the child shape the way the child will think when the child becomes an adult. One of the main ways in which this happens is when the child observes the mother's reaction to abuse. Here are three typical reactions that abused women exhibit:

a.   She does not know that she is being abused. She may have learnt from her family or her culture that a wife is a slave to the husband, or that physical, emotional or sexual abuse are part of the "normal pattern" in a marriage. She believes that she must bear the abuse patiently, even though she herself may develop mental and physical health issues.

b.   She may resent it, try her best to stop it, but finally decide to stay in the abusive situation due to considerations like her children's future or financial constraints.

c.   She might have put up with the abuse initially, but

finally separates from the abuser.

In most cases, the victim (ironically, by her sheer endurance) reinforces the belief that abuse is a part of life, and the child internalizes this belief. In cases of separation, if the child's needs are not considered and the child is left with the abuser or with step-parents, the child suffers from a lack of love and an overwhelming feeling of emptiness.

3. The Repetitive Stage

Many children who are exposed to abuse at the hands of or between their parents, grow into adulthood severely deprived of love, as the parents are not able to provide the secure foundation that their child needs. The abuse gets reinforced in their minds and the cycle begins to repeat itself. The child becomes either an abuser, imposing violence on one's partner, or a victim, accepting abuse as a lifestyle. If the child is a boy who has grown in a patriarchal society, he tends to grow up to be abusive because he believes abuse is acceptable within the context of marriage. If the child is a girl, she prefers to stay in a long-term, abusive marriage, and later reinforces abuse for her children, because she has grown up to believe that abuse in marriage is normal and inevitable.

VINEET'S STORY

As a child, Vineet often saw his father hitting his mother. He never saw his mother defending herself or fighting back. Instead, she kept making excuses for her husband's abusive behavior. Vineet often walked into the house just when his mother was getting thrashed and verbally abused. His father would even invite him to join in the hitting and abusing. Vineet would break down crying and run into the next room in fear. As he grew up, his attitude towards girls changed completely. Once, when he was teased by a girl in school, he hit her and was suspended from school for a day.

He met and married Pallavi, who had been a close friend of his. When Pallavi said something that triggered his anger, he grabbed her throat and started pounding her head against the wall. Pallavi was beaten every time Vineet felt that she had stepped out of line. He once pushed her so hard that she ended up breaking her ankle and she hid his abuse by lying to the neighbors. He provoked her unendingly and when she reacted, he was happy because he had an excuse to teach her a lesson with his fists. Pallavi was constantly abused over the years and, in her heart, she honestly believed that the beatings and verbal abuse were a normal part of every marriage. Pallavi continued to face abuse, even after becoming the mother of three children. As in the case of Vineet's childhood, the children looked on as their father beat their mother. They started seeing abuse as a part of marriage as well. When the children grew up and had spouses of their own, it was not long before the daughter started getting abused by her husband and the son became an abuser like his father.

RANJEET'S STORY

Ranjeet's parents' marriage was volatile and violent, with repeated episodes of his mother walking out. Whenever the abuse escalated, his mother would suddenly disappear for hours and then reappear. After a particular big fight between the parents, his mother left behind a suicide note and disappeared. Ranjeet's little heart was filled with fear and his terrifying screams brought his neighbors to his home. They organized a search party and found her near the seashore, walking alone at night.

When he was just nine years old, Ranjeet started to worry a great deal about his mother. His school teachers saw in him a sad, angry and nervous little boy, who often seemed more frightened than depressed. At times, he was withdrawn and sullen; at other times, he would bully his classmates. When his mother finally walked out, he went along with her and, over time, he had a string of step-fathers. Ranjeet took it upon himself to defend his mother against some of her more violent partners. He even took out a knife once and threatened to kill one of her partners, saying, "You are not going to hurt my mummy." Finally, he started believing that he had become invincible. He bullied others aggressively and he started stealing, lying and fighting, eventually ending up in a juvenile home.

THE ORIGIN OF ABUSE

1. Many who become abusers have invariably witnessed a lot of abuse and pain as children. Children, who watch abuse being played out on a daily basis, tend to repress their painful childhood memories. All this hurt, anger and pain come tumbling out when the abused child reaches breaking point as an adult.

2. Some children who come from families that enjoy healthy relationships become abusers when they witness abusive relationships of friends and relatives. Seeing the control and power wielded by the abuser makes them want to try their hand at being a dominant and aggressive person. For e.g., Raju's parents were very loving at home. But, at his school, he had a circle of friends who had bad habits. This group of boys thrived on asserting their manhood by talking down to girls. They encouraged in Raju the belief that if he liked a girl, he needed to aggressively pursue her, because girls secretly liked "bad boys." Never questioning their advice, Raju followed the belief of his friends. He was proud of his "bad boy" image and didn't think twice about raising his hand against girls. When he got married, he became an abusive and angry husband. Given his environmental influences, one is not surprised.

3.   Many children become abusers if they were victims of constant bullying by their classmates and peers. Bullying causes low self-esteem and a severe inferiority complex. As they grow up, these children start toughening up and hide their inferiority issues by putting on an aggressive and angry front. They are not receptive to love. As men, they abuse their wives constantly, to gain a sense of control. For e.g., Tom's parents were extremely loving people. Tom was academically weak and was of a small build. His teachers kept punishing him when he fared badly in his studies, which was very often. To add to his humiliation, his friends kept making fun of his height and small frame. Tom was scared to stand up for himself and was bullied for years. He bottled his anger up and was like a pressure cooker waiting to explode. Once he got married, his wife became the outlet for all his pent-up emotions. He beat her on a daily basis and found fault with everything she said and did. She was often covered with bruises from the beatings and had to lie to her relatives about how she had obtained them. After years and years of beatings and fights, she just accepted the abuse as her lot in life.

IF YOU WERE ABUSED AS A CHILD, DON'T REPRESS THE EMOTIONS

If you were abused as a child, don't repress the emotions. Though you may not become an abuser or a victim, repression of memories can turn inward, causing severe depression.

TO BREAK THAT CYCLE

As the pattern of abuse is subconscious learning from

childhood, it can definitely be unlearned. One needs to recognize it and make a conscious effort to break it. This vicious cycle keeps getting transferred from one generation to another, and won't stop until someone in a particular generation decides to break free. To find out why it is very hard for the abused to break out of an abusive relationship, and why the abuser does not easily allow the victim to go, we should answer two questions: Why does she stay? And why does he abuse?

Why Does She Stay?

An abuser does not look like a tough guy with angry eyes, as people tend to imagine. He could be the most educated, respected and friendly of people and, because of this, the victim finds it difficult to understand that she is being abused. The more educated and intelligent an abuser is, the more difficult the victim finds it to leave, because of his ability to convince her and others that the abuse is because of her. Everyone may have different opinions about him. For example, his sister and mother might say that he is the most affectionate person in the world, his pastor might regard him as the gentlest human being, and his friend might say that everyone gets angry at times and this is just a passing phase in his life due to office stress. All these lead the victim to denial, confusion, self-blame, and feelings of worthlessness, despair, and guilt. Many victims end up feeling that they deserved it. Some of the victims stay because of the fear of landing in the streets or losing their children if they leave, as their abuser would have isolated them from family and friends, so that he can be their only provider. Many victims are terrorized and traumatized to the extent that they are scared to leave for fear of character assassination or even of being hurt and killed. The abused stays with the abuser because they feel powerless and worthless, and believe they deserve nothing more than abuse.

But Why Does An Abuser Abuse?

Is he born an abuser? Is abuse his aim? Is he a monster? The answer is an emphatic no! In most cases, the abuser abuses so that he can remain powerful and get all his needs met. In the abuser's mind, the woman should not have any need of her own, and she just exists as a personal caretaker to cater to all his needs. He expects his partner to keep him on a high pedestal by doing all that he wishes and appreciating everything he does. When this does not happen, he feels that he has the right to get what he wants by using abuse and manipulation. Since he is never satisfied, his demands keep escalating, and the victim feels that she can never satisfy him. The partner looks like an object in the mind of an abuser, and so he can deal cruelly with her with no empathy or guilt. Since the abuser feels that he owns his partner, he treats her in a degrading manner, and monitors her every activity, showering her with hurtful accusations.

How To Break The Cycle?

If you are a victim, the first step to breaking the cycle of abuse is to recognize that you are being abused. Never put yourself in an abusive environment because you rely on the abuser for basic needs like food and shelter. Recognize the abusive patterns and the warning signs of the abuser. Ignore the abusive statements intended to malign and demean, and learn to defuse them. Understand that you are not at fault and ignore the guilt trips that the abuser tries to put you through.

If you are abusing your partner, you too can break the cycle. Get counselling and work on the negative experiences from your past, by talking to a trained therapist and focusing on inner healing. Grieve for what has been lost and find constructive ways to overcome the effects of abuse. Without intervention, abuse tends to escalate. Seek assistance from support groups or NGOs that deal with issues of domestic violence. In a review article, Priscilla Schulz writes about a study conducted among men who participated in a 20-week group treatment for batterers at Changing Ways Inc., in London, Ontario, Canada [9]. Nine men met the criteria to become study participants as these men had succeeded in "changing abusive behavior through treatment" and had maintained that change for at least six months before the study. The participants, their intimate partners and their counselors evaluated the success of these men in changing abusive behavior. There was a general agreement between the participants' perceptions of what helped them change and the theories of abuse development and behavior change now prevalent. Four factors stood out as most important to the men in changing their abusive behavior. Seventy-five percent of the men endorsed the following factors:

1. Recognizing and taking responsibility for past abusive behavior.

2. Developing empathy for others, most specifically for intimate partners, when participants came to understand how fear, intimidation and the cumulative effect of "controlling behaviors" had affected their relationships with intimate partners.

3. Reducing dependency; accepting sole responsibility for change in abusive behavior, and understanding that their intimate partners were autonomous beings with rights to feelings and making decisions, and to having privacy about those feelings and decisions.

4. Improving skills for communicating needs, feelings

and other difficult topics(most importantly, anger management, and conflict management and resolution), learning how to listen to partners during difficult discussions, and learning how to share feelings and have intimate conversations.

FOR A BETTER TOMORROW

No matter how healthy a marriage is, a couple will have the occasional fight or argument. Though it's pretty normal for couples to fight, there should be certain boundaries that neither should cross. If one partner says hurtful, abusive and vindictive things to the other partner, after they cool down, the couple needs to sit down and ensure that the injured partner shares their hurt regarding the uncalled-for comments.

If these fights continue, then the couple needs to immediately seek counseling. But, in an abusive relationship, the abuser has the skill to playact the role of a truly reformed person convincingly, even with the counselor. The counselor might buy his act and advise the wife to take him back. The wife does so in good faith and it's not long before the abuse starts again. The abuser should be made to recognize that if his behavior continues to be abusive, he may end up losing his marriage or even end up in jail. If the abuser understands the effect of his behavior on his victim, takes responsibility for his behavior, and is accountable for his behavior, there is hope for transformation.

Parents need to remember that their children are vulnerable, and will need to see counselors or therapists to deal with the trauma of their parents getting divorced or of witnessing violence in an abusive environment. If the children were victims of abuse or have witnessed battering at home, these memories can prevent them from growing up into whole individuals. Regular counseling can help them in the healing process. Children should be taught that abuse must not be tolerated and that everyone has the right to a life of dignity. Even though parents might be at loggerheads with each other, they should never poison their children's impressionable minds by saying nasty things about each other. Parents who force the child to take sides, put the child in a very difficult position. Custody and visitation are difficult issues and parents need to constantly keep their children's best interests in mind.

Assuring your child of your love, can bring healing. After all, they are truly the only legacy that matters. The best way to do this is to try and work through all the problems of an abusive marriage, to see if there is hope to save it. Sometimes you may need to measure out some rope and give the abuser a chance to change and get help, before slamming the brakes on a relationship.

CHAPTER FOUR

To Measure the Rope

*"Freedom is never voluntarily given by the oppressor; it must be
demanded by the oppressed."*

— *Martin Luther King, Jr.*

A couple doesn't need to consider divorce at the very first sign of abuse. Repairing a relationship tainted or even damaged by abuse can be hard. Time, energy, and patience are absolutely essential in restoring the relationship, by rebuilding trust and intimacy.

Can every marriage be saved? What if a victim wants to save her marriage but needs protection? How can an abused wife assess if her husband can really change (with the help of society, counselors, through trials, separation, etc)? How long should the rope be, that's let out to an abusive husband, in the hope of his transformation? At which point should the rope be cut off?

ROPE TEST: WHEN IT'S A GAMBLE

Marriage was always meant to be a commitment between two people who deeply care about each other and a good marriage creates an environment that is conducive to bringing up children. It must be protected, at all costs. But, if a marriage consists of constant arguments or fights, and there is no sign that the abusive spouse will change his behavior, it is dangerous for a woman and her children to remain in such a situation. Often, the precious marriage covenant needs to be shredded, to protect the life and sanity of the wife and children. One should not allow the abuse to continue at the cost of vain attempts to protect the marriage. The opposite is also true: the marriage must not be hastily dissolved, if there might be a chance for healing and restoration, through counseling and therapy.

A couple doesn't need to consider divorce at the very first sign of abuse. Repairing a relationship tainted or even damaged by abuse can be hard. Time, energy, and patience are absolutely essential in restoring the relationship, by rebuilding trust and intimacy. If the abuser realizes that his behavior towards his partner was inexcusable and if she is given the space to freely express her thoughts and emotions, without fearing intimidation or threats, then it should be okay for the victim to stay in the marriage.

DUELING ROPES: DISPENSE WITH THE VERBAL SWORDS

"S!@$%!#%$&%#&%*&*&$%*(%^" are choice words that
spring automatically from some angry husbands. Many
people think verbal abuse is a normal part of marriage. But,
words do cause significant damage and those who have
suffered their lashes know that they can be as injurious as
physical blows to the body. Destructive though it is, this
problem can be dealt with permanently, if the person is
willing to change and be honest about his shortcomings.
Both the partners must carefully measure the words and
tone they use at all times, and it is important to remember
that in most cases, verbal abuse precedes physical abuse. In
such cases, it is better to change vocabulary than to break a
marriage.

ROPE IN YOUR FACE: DON'T LOOK THE OTHER WAY

Has there been a time when a young wife has walked into
the office with a badly bruised face, claiming that it was
the result of an untimely door accident, and her colleagues
have accepted her story? Most people know that the young
wife's tale is a blatant lie and that she has been a victim
of physical abuse. Yet, somehow, it seems convenient to
accept her story and avoid getting involved. After all, each
one of us has problems in life—a special child, an alcoholic
parent, a wayward brother, or an unfaithful husband.
So, there is generally little inclination to bear another's
burden. You are not going to be proud if this desperate
young wife commits suicide someday. We need to step out
of our comfort zones, when there is someone in our life
who needs support.

Why is the victim trying to conceal the abuse? It could
be one of several reasons:

1.   She may be in complete denial or might be confused

about whether she provoked the attack;

2. She may fear the consequences of exposing the abuse;

3. Most of all, she may be overwhelmed with embarrassment, shame, loss of self-image or deception.

DON'T MOPE OVER THIS ROPE: DISORDERS AS EXCUSES

It is true that many abusers suffer from personality disorders like Bipolar Disorder, Schizophrenia, Narcissism, Chemical Dependency or Alcoholism. Such people are the most severe of abusers, using their psychological issues as an excuse for violence. A victim must not be taken in by this pretext. She is well within her rights to walk out of the harmful circumstance and seek safety for her children and herself. For all that she knows, her brave decision might inspire the abuser to change. The abuser should be confronted with the reality that he will lose something of great value if he does not change. If he suffers from psychological problems, he has to undergo treatment—there can be no other option. If he refuses, do not play the martyr. It is better for the wife to leave than to give her husband any more opportunity to abuse her. Every victimized wife must remember that the recognition of abuse is the first move towards the healing.

REPAIRING A RELATIONSHIP TAINTED OR EVEN DAMAGED BY ABUSE CAN BE HARD.

ROPE RESEARCH: TO LEAVE?

Situation Assessment

I deeply sympathize with wives who are at crossroads, wondering whether they are ruining their own lives by walking out of their marriages. Their minds constantly churn up ways in which they can change their abusive husbands.

Dearest one, if your partner abuses you, the abuse is not going to stop until he deals with his issues. It is out of your control. You can only change what is within your reach. If years have passed and you haven't been able to effect much change in him, inform him that you are going to leave him. Normally, abusers don't take steps to change unless they hit rock bottom. Once they realize that the victim is determined to leave, they might become even more abusive. Many even threaten suicide or murder.

On the other hand, when you inform him about the separation or divorce, if he does not respond with hostility and opens up to the idea of changing his ways, then there is hope. You can cautiously reconsider and put a temporary brake on your plans to leave. Make him take responsibility for his actions and work together to find solutions that satisfy both of you.

In some cases, it might not be abuse at all. It maybe just an obsession brought about by an inferiority complex, and properly dealing with this issue can save the marriage. The perfect example for such a situation is the one my friend Sujatha and her husband found themselves in.

From the beginning of their marriage, Sujatha's husband Shantaram was consumed with suspicion. When she went to work or if she received a phone call at home, he had doubts about what she was doing. He was convinced that there were many men vying for her affection and that she was having affairs with some of them. His suspicions were groundless but the more he thought about them, the more the fears multiplied, and suspicion began to control his behavior. He even began visiting some of her friends, just to find out more about her activities. Sujatha got to hear about her husband's "jealousy" but she would laugh it off because she was a person of integrity and she had done nothing wrong.

However, once when she found out that he had been standing near her office, trying to spy on her, she was furious and thought of leaving him. She confronted him, and was surprised when he burst into tears. He then revealed a letter he had received, which was obviously written by a vindictive colleague, who had been denied the promotion that went to Sujatha. Shantaram did not want to lose Sujatha, so he agreed to her suggestion of marriage counseling. It was during those sessions that she discovered that her husband suffered from low self-esteem and had an inferiority complex because she was tall and fair while he was dark and plain looking; he had been constantly fearful that she would leave him because the men in her workplace looked better than him.

After appropriate counseling, during which both the partners decided to work together to save their marriage, they became a truly happy couple.

> THE FIRST STEP TO BE FREE FROM ABUSE IS BASED ON HOW REALISTICALLY YOU CAN EVALUATE YOUR RELATIONSHIP

ASSESS THE RELATIONSHIP

The first step to be free from abuse is based on how realistically you can evaluate your relationship, by examining and assessing the precise nature of the abuse you are undergoing. Move away from all emotions and think logically. Do not whip yourself if you feel confused: remember that people who have abusive partners have long since stopped thinking logically. Take time alone, away from the influence of the abuser.

Take a pencil and paper and do an honest, dispassionate assessment on whether life in the household is becoming worse day by day, and whether by sticking on you are endangering your life and sanity. Divide the page into two:

on one side, list the reasons for staying in the marriage, and the other, the reasons you want out. Below, I have mentioned some things you can do to get started.

- ### Record of Abusive Behavior

  Write down, without embellishment, the behavior of your abuser, the severity and the frequency of abusive incidents, the violence meted out to you, and the lies and dirty words used by him. If you were forced into physical intimacy after such behavior, write that down as well. List all the humiliating, frightening and traumatic events during your time with your spouse.

- ### The Debilitating Effect

  Write down the effects of such abuse: diminished worth, impact on your health, your sleep and your appetite. If basic human needs like respect, emotional security, trust and a serene life were absent, then write a declaration to that effect.

- ### Impact on Children

  Note down any abnormal behavior you saw in them: disrespect, anger, withdrawal, etc. Note incidents when they have felt compelled to play the abuser's or victim's role.

- ### Times of Danger

  Make a record of any physical injuries you may have sustained in these abusive encounters. Avoid exaggeration while writing down these details.

- ### The Better Side

  Many abusers are good with children and take care of the family, despite their abusive nature. They may be very good fathers and may spend quality time with the children. Write down the good characteristics of your partner. Write down whether he feels real remorse after he has hurt you. List the positive incidents your life—times when he has demonstrated love and you have enjoyed the relationship.

- *If You Stay*

  Your life, health, self-esteem, respect, children's respect, children's character, children's peace of mind—list all the things you are likely to lose if you stay on in the relationship.

- *If You Leave*

  List the things you will lose if you walk away. You might not have money to support yourself and your children; your friends might leave you; there could be strong opposition from religious leaders; you might have to face the anger of your children, etc.

At the end of such an evaluative exercise, you will find your decision. The decision to leave or stay should not be taken on the spur of a moment. Be completely honest with yourself. Though emotional abuse deadens the soul and poisons the mind, if you are sure that your life is not in danger, you can plan to stay on and try to redeem the situation. If the children's minds are not polluted by the abuser, and provided you can find ways to explain to the children what is happening in the home, then you may want to consider sorting the issues out. (Make sure you tell them only as much as they can absorb.)

THE ROPE DANCE: JUST ONE MORE CHANCE

It had gone on for more years than she could count. He would beat her severely at night, and in the morning, he would be full of tears and apologies. "I'll never do it again," he'd say. A couple of days later, a thrashing much worse than before would follow. "Please forgive me! I have no one," he'd plead. Once, when her hand got fractured, she packed up to go to her parents' house. "If you leave me, I'll die! I'll kill myself! I promise you, it will never happen again," he'd said, amidst sobs. A few days later, he pushed her down the stairs. Another time, he took a stick and, beat her, and then cursed himself for being cruel to a wife who was a perfect angel.

In the usual abusive environment, many chances are given to the abuser by the victim, in the desperate hope that he will change. She is in total denial. Even though her hope runs dry, one victim protested, "It's not denial. Till the day I die, I will pray for him to change." Little does this poor woman know that if the abuse keeps escalating, then that day will not be far off. She may be deceiving herself by working towards being more perfect, loving and forgiving, and this incredibly complex concept keeps her going. Misplaced hope and denial are a deadly combination.

It is not unusual to hope that your spouse will change into the person you need him to be. However, this hope of changing another is futile. You keep thinking that if you both go for counseling, things will change, or once he stops drinking or leaves the other woman or becomes religious, it'll work out. The problem with this is that it keeps you away from reality and you may end up waiting a lifetime. Making the choice of letting go of an abusive marriage is really hard, but in the end, you find that it may be an opportunity for a new beginning.

Ladies, let me tell you one thing. Few violent men have changed, when they have gotten away with being abusive for years. When these violent men have not been made accountable by relatives, colleagues, friends, police, or society, their abuse is being enabled by the people around them. Why should they change? They have gotten away with it successfully for so long. It's the perfect setup for their broken personalities to vent out their insecurities.

On the other hand, there are situations where confrontations by victims in front of relatives or counselors, cause the abusers to shift blame or avoid the topic. There have even been cases where abusers have managed to convince people that such things have never happened and that the poor delusional wife is simply trying to paint him black.

THEN, THERE IS THIS AMAZING MAJORITY THAT ACCEPTS THE TRUTH OF THE VICTIM'S ACCOUNT BUT CLAIMS THAT THE "DISCIPLINING" IS FOR THE BENEFIT OF THE WIVES

Then, there is this amazing majority that accepts the truth of the victim's account but claims that the "disciplining" is for the benefit of the wives. I have found it astounding that when I have sometimes helped a victim value her life and seek change, the other people in her life counter the advice given and beg the victim to give the abuser another chance. It is also frustrating to see women staying with severely abusive partners just because they are excellent providers; the victims do this out of fear of homelessness and poverty if they choose to leave. It is time to decide what is most important to you: your and your children's lives or your comfort zone?

My dear, if you are being abused and are confused by these strategies, I don't blame you. However, please don't delay because the abuse will escalate. I hope that you would give some serious consideration to my advice. Better flee before the abuse becomes life threatening.

AKHILA'S STORY

Her husband was an important man in the local government. When he began to ill-treat her, she had the gumption to take her two sons and leave the house. Then she began to approach the courts to get him to pay maintenance for the children and herself. The court decreed that he must pay. He never did. She joined a single parent association and often whined that her husband was doing so well while she and her sons were eking out a meager existence. She wanted to know what harsh action she could take against her husband. The counselor in the association confronted her with this solution: "Instead of expending your energy pursuing him to give you money he does not want to and perhaps never will give, why don't you use that same energy to discover your skills and build up a new life for yourself?"

When Akhila walked out of the meeting, the counselor wondered if she had been too harsh, since Akhila didn't attend many meetings after that incident.

Eighteen months later, a brand new Akhila walked into the meeting. She was radiant. Since her husband had been in the construction business and that was all she knew, she had approached her siblings for large loans, which she promised she'd return with interest, within two years. Immediately after she got the money together, she approached every related contact she had from her married life and used their help to construct a four storeyed building, in a commercial area. For one year, she worked daily from 5.30 am in the morning till sunset, to personally supervise the construction. At nights, she checked the accounts while helping her sons with their studies. Akhila said to the counselor, "I took your advice. Today, I have just leased out the final section of my building. I now have an income of six+ lakhs every month." Everybody clapped and Akhila's story encouraged several despairing single mothers there.

ROPE IN FLIGHT: WHEN THE BEST OPTION IS LEAVING

If you have decided to walk out, plan some safeguards and start preparing yourself months before you actually walk out. Familiarize yourself with domestic abuse laws and gather as much evidence as possible. Document the abuse by keeping a daily journal of every abusive incident you experience, be it physical or emotional abuse, with details like dates and circumstances. Whenever there is a black eye, cut or bruise involved, take photos, and go to an emergency room or a mental health clinic immediately, so that you have medical records to support your claim. Call the police and file an FIR with every single instance of abuse. Tell as many people as possible. Inform relatives, neighbors and colleagues. The more witnesses you have, the stronger your case will be, should the need arise. If your partner is obsessed about you, the situation might become very dangerous. An obsessive man cannot handle the thought of losing the "object" that he possesses and it can drive him to stalk, harass, or threaten his victim. This can even result in a homicide or suicide. Women, who find themselves in such a situation, need to inform their families and must keep the police in the loop, if necessary. If the violence escalates, you can file a restraining order, prohibiting the abuser's entry into the house. Then the abuser has to stay away, because on violation of the order, you can have him arrested. List the people you can count on for support in an emergency. Also, mentally prepare yourself by constantly remembering that you are not alone, and that you can face this difficult situation with the help of God. A few points to help you in times of emergency are listed below:

- *If there is a medical emergency:* If you are severely bleeding or any bones have been broken and you are rushed to the hospital, remember that many abusers follow their victims into treatment rooms, to make sure their victims don't expose them. They may force the victims to report the injury as an accident or a fall. If this happens to you, send your spouse to the car or medical shop or canteen, on the pretext of getting something, so that you can confide with the doctor there. Medical records should be based on facts. Do not take a bath or change clothing before seeking medical attention. Keep torn or bloody clothing and photograph your injuries. Call the police and report your attack.

- *If you are being stalked:* Try to obtain a work transfer to another geographic location. This way, you can move to the security and safety of another city, while making the decision on the permanent move you are going to make. Start storing records in a safe place. Research your legal rights to seek counseling. Try to contact NGOs and government agencies working on domestic violence for support.

- *If you are taken hostage:* If there is a possibility of your abuser getting to know that you are seriously considering leaving, the situation could turn dangerous. Establish a connection with a neighbor or a friend early on and request them to look out (should danger strike) for a visible signal, like flashing an SOS by turning a light switch on and off a number of times, so that they can contact the police to help you.

- *If space is what you need:* Choose a non-threatening reason like visiting a friend who is far away, or a relative who is sick, to get some time away by yourself. This time away from your abuser will give you the space needed to think more clearly. The temporary separation can defuse escalated anger and can help to permanently separate with lesser conflict.

TEARS IN THE ROPE: BEYOND FORGIVENESS

My heart aches as I write this. Life cannot be easily erased. The adage "forgive and forget" sounds sensible but only a victim of abuse can certify how unhelpful that is. You have been scarred by someone you love, so your heart aches and you wear a plastic smile. But, behind that smile is a world of pain. The inner scrutiny tends to be relentless: why did this happen? Was it divine punishment? For what?

After finally having walked out of an abusive situation, many victims are left outside in a cold, hostile and unloving world, with their children, with no finances and with their bodies and minds struggling to regain normalcy. They find themselves unable to reconcile with the past and, when a wave of emptiness sweeps over them, it is almost impossible for them to heal and they inevitably give in to

FORGIVE A WIFE-SLAMMER IF YOU CAN. BUT YOU DON'T HAVE TO LIVE WITH HIM

depression. Many victims have complained that during the night, the memories fill them with dread and blinding fear.

Lewis Smedes, claims that forgiveness is possible as he writes, "To forgive is to set a prisoner free and discover that the prisoner was you [10]." I also strongly believe that forgiveness is a wise choice because it sets the mind free from the torment of the past. But, forgiveness, trust, and reconciliation are all different issues. Again Lewis Smedes says poignantly, "We don't have to tolerate what people do just because we forgive them for doing it. Forgiving heals us personally. To tolerate everything only hurts us all in the long run [11]."

Smedes' most significant words are:

"Forgive a wife-slammer if you can. But you don't have to live with him. Forgive a husband who is abusing your children if you can. But only after you kick him out of the house. And if you can't get him out, get help. It's available. In the meantime, don't let him near the kids, and don't let anyone tell you that if you forgive him it means you have to stay with him."

This reality has caused me immense grief. Many victims of domestic violence leave the abuser only after they have been permanently disfigured, emotionally and physically. I have come face-to-face with women who have lost their arms, who have had their spines broken or who have been badly burnt. How could I find the audacity to ask these victims to forgive their offenders? Trapped in helplessness and despair, the victim rages at the world, as she stands there in stark pain. At such times, it seems impossible for the victim to forgive the offender. In *"Abba's Child: The Cry of the Heart for Intimate Belonging,"* Brennan Manning says "… forces greater than ourselves can empower us to forgive the wounds inflicted by others."

Beloved, if you have been irreparably wronged and wounded, please give yourself time and space to heal and keep in mind that it is a long process. However, I plead with you to forgive your offender so that you can change the memory of your past into a hope for your future. With God's help, anything is possible.

FUTURE ROPE: HOPE
Here is an example that will inspire you.

I don't want to go into the graphic details of why I landed at the divorce courts, but after the divorce my life was falling apart.

My husband said that since I had decided to leave him, we should have a mutual divorce and that we could use the same lawyer. Since we went through a mutual divorce, I couldn't ask for any child support but I had decided to leave it to him to provide for the two children. At that moment, I began to hide in my house. I felt like everybody was looking at me.

I want to give credit to my older brother. When my mother told him that I was becoming a recluse, he took leave from work and from his family, and came to be with me. He spent one month with me. I cannot get over it. My self-confidence was at an all-time low. My husband had always called me a "useless bitch" and I believed him. But, my brother came up with a plan—to get me out of depression and into the real world. He was like a ray of sunshine at home. He joked and played with the kids.

He somehow forced me to admit that I was interested in filmmaking. One of my friends was a TV film producer and she had told me how exciting her job was. I thought that that was something I might be able to do well. That was all that my brother needed. He disappeared for the two next days and searched the city for a media school.

He found a media school that offered a two-year TV production course and ensured that I enrolled in it before he left. He insisted on sponsoring me, telling me that I should view it just as a loan (he knew that I was not the kind to accept gifts or borrow money from others). For two years, it was as if my brother had conspired with God to give me something so beautiful. My children were in school and the classes were for four hours each day, between 11 am to 3 pm. So I was able to attend classes regularly, and complete my assignments and research work at home, while my children were at school. I had explained my personal situation to a few people in my class and all of them were supportive and cooperative.

To cut a long story short, within three years, my son had completed his schooling and was getting ready to join a professional stream, and I had gotten a job as a producer's assistant. They saw something innovative and creative in me. After a few years, I became a film producer. I shared everything with my children. So they were a part of the whole process. They were so excited. It took our minds off of the loneliness of them living without their father. The important point which I want to share with other women who go through a divorce is that I concentrated on the future. I was very positive. I made it a point to see that I never blackened my husband's name with my children. I know that children need both of their parents, a father and a mother, no matter what the father may have done.

The good thing is that my ex-husband made a lot of time for the children (even though he had remarried and had another child with his new wife) and I gave him full access to them. I didn't play any games by stopping their meetings. Initially, I tried attending single parent groups but found that many of them were contaminated by their hatred towards men. They wanted to hate men; they bashed men at their meetings. I didn't want to do that and didn't want such thoughts entering my mind. So I sorted these things out with myself. I am grateful to my brother for helping me find my way back to a full life.

Today, I'm a successful TV producer. There is nothing in the world like a good marriage. However, if your marriage has died, if it is rotting and destroying two people, then it is better that they separate. A dead marriage needs to be buried; otherwise, like a dead body, it stinks up the environment of a home.

Divorce, they tell me, does not have to be the end of the road; it might just herald a promising new future.

CHAPTER FIVE

When The Rope Tears

"Leaving an abusive partner is a very difficult thing to do. It frequently feels like you are failing, or destroying your family, or not trying to work things out, or not giving your partner 'a second chance.' It hurts, and it's scary."

— Blaine Nelson

*E*ven your own family starts treating you differently. They love you but when they see you, they see failure. Parents perceive divorce as personal failure and would have preferred a bad marriage to a broken marriage.

Life sometimes does not turn out the way we plan or pray about. As more rope length is given, many times the grip on life gets lost. The rope tears and divorce happens. Any other word is preferred—heartbreak, failure, anguish, rupture or even wreck. But Divorce? That seems like a bit too much to handle. When the rope tears, maybe it's time to just let go; it may be time for a new start.

Make no mistake. One of the best forms of happiness found on earth is a happy marriage. There is nothing that can equal the joy that flows from the union of a man and a woman. It is the way the Almighty intended it to be; to start a new family, which will multiply joys and divide sorrows. Whether through an arrangement or through Cupid's mischief, many marriages work their way through thorns and bristles to plant rose gardens with inspiring resolutions. The husband loves and cares for the wife, and the wife, on her part, is devoted to her man and handles the pressures of running the house and bringing up the children.

Sex is more than just a physical activity—it is the spiritual amalgamation of two bodies within one another, a testament to the love and devotion between a husband and wife. It's not that conflict won't happen from time to time. There will be arguments, misunderstandings, and disagreements over minor and major things. But, mutual love and common ambition for family welfare helps the husband and wife to patch things up, before the sun sets each day.

So, every marriage creates its own little paradise on earth, and the husband and wife seem to find their own happily ever after, as they walk off into the sunset. Beautiful Picture! There are very few things on earth that equal the joy of a well-aligned, happy marriage.

What about the Ugly Picture? Broken dreams, crushed spirit, bottomless agony, black eye, fractured limb, shattered ribs, terrified children, monstrous ravings, public shame, and no hope in sight?

Yes, I agree with those who say that divorce is worse than the death of a loved one, as it lacks the finality of death. As a matter of fact, few would dispute the fact that widows are viewed and treated with more compassion than divorcees. But, when there is no other option left, one must make this decision, despite the stigma. One can't possibly forget that the husband, wife and children, will all suffer the consequences of that decision. While the divorced couple understands the conscious decision they have made, the children are left in a lurch, confused and terrified.

To really understand what I mean, consider a small, slightly thick, branch of a tree. Now, snap it in two with your fingers. You will discover that it is not a perfect break; it is impossible for the stick to snap into two evenly split pieces. Instead, you are left with two jagged pieces. The same happens when a couple is divorced. Much as they may want to make a clean break, for their own sakes and for the sake of their children, they discover that it is wishful thinking. There are many jagged pieces that pull them back into a proximity they wish to avoid—children, assets, resources, judicially apportioned shared custody, and above all, families and friends from both sides! In India, marriage is never between two persons but two families. Likewise, divorce is also a family affair; a divorce takes place between two families. Parents and cousins of both partners are forced on either side of the fence, and it isn't long before the mudslinging starts.

Before we get into the various other aspects of separating assets and relatives, let's deal with the effects of divorce and the toll it takes on its victims. Without holding back, I would like to reveal the full picture of what a divorce involves, so that you can make an educated and informed decision. Once again, I would like to emphatically state that I do not propagate divorce. A good marriage is a longing that is deeply embedded in the hearts of most people who breathe.

But, in cases like repeated infidelity or physical battering coupled with emotional abuse, divorce is the preferred option, owing to the impending risk of losing one's life and the devastating effects of abuse on innocent children. Of course, when a divorce takes place, children are negatively affected. But it doesn't compare with their precarious condition in a household traumatized by an abusive father.

To help you gain a comprehensive overview of divorce, I have broken down everything that needs to be said on the topic into five sections. Valuable lessons are also provided through the stories of women who have grappled with life after divorce. These stories give precious glimpses into what some women did, what they went through and how they came to terms with life, after the judge hit the gavel on the walnut hardwood sound-block and declared, "This marriage is dissolved and terminated!"

GIVE THE TAG THE SLIP

Maneka Gandhi was once interviewed by Ingrid Albuquerque for SAVVY, one of India's leading women's magazines. An excerpt from that interview is given below..

I: *Maneka, how did your life change once you became a widow?*

M: *I have never seen myself as a widow.*

I: *A woman who loses her husband to death is usually called a widow.*

M: A woman will be called what she chooses to be called. I decided what I preferred not to be called.

I: So if not as a widow, how do you see yourself? How do you describe yourself?

M: I put it very simply. I was a woman who had a husband. Now I do not have a husband. I say it in exactly those words. I will not use the word widow because it comes with a lot of excess baggage, either of unwanted sympathy or of making yourself vulnerable to be deplored, pitied or exploited by society.

IF YOU DO NOT WANT TO BE CALLED A DIVORCEE, ENSURE YOU DO NOT EVER REFER TO YOURSELF THAT WAY AND DO NOT LET ANYONE CALL YOU THAT EITHER

For those abused wives who are terrified of the label "divorcee," and sometimes prefer to stay in rotten circumstances in fear of that, Maneka's approach can be adopted. Let's face it: no woman is born with the ambition of wanting to be a divorcee. If after legally snapping ties with an abusive husband, you do not want to be called a divorcee, ensure you do not ever refer to yourself that way and do not let anyone call you that either.

If you are asked about your marital status, simply say, "I had a husband before, but I do not have one now. But I am raising two wonderful children."

If the interrogation persists: "What happened to your husband? Did he die?" simply reply, "No."

If the questioner continues, "Are you a divorcee?," simply respond with "I prefer not to use the word."

Perhaps, at this stage, you could reach out, touch her hand in an appeal, and gently say, "I'd prefer not to share anymore, but please do pray for me and my children."

Maneka is right. The world will see you as you see yourself and you are the only one who can etch your profile and erect your personal boundaries. No matter what the provocation, don't feel any compulsion to expose your story or make yourself vulnerable. Be careful of candid confessions in groups. If you are with people who suddenly break into exchanging intimate details about their personal life, silently move away from that group. It would not be fair to listen to their confessions, since you will not be sharing yours. I advise you not to bare details of your life early in the journey as a divorcee because your emotions may still be raw and you might say things that you might not want to be tagged with later.

ARMED FOR A BATTLE

Anyone who tells you that it's possible to whizz through a divorce easily, needs help themselves. Divorce is a very difficult period, even for a strongest and most resilient person. In the aftermath of a divorce:

- Though friends, relatives and well-wishers may have been encouraging before, most of these people usually vanish.

- Lest you should ask them to house your children and you, many "close friends" will soon be inaccessible to you.

- You may face increased opposition from family, if you come from a traditional and authoritarian background, where obedience to one's husband is considered paramount. Parents often perceive divorce as personal failure, and prefer a bad marriage to a broken marriage. The extended family will start treating you differently as well; they love you, but when they see you, they see failure.

- In many cases, the religious community turns against divorcees, so you may not find any support from it. Your friends, relatives and immediate family members might perceive you as being proud and arrogant, as trying to rebel against your husband.

- Many previously sympathetic wives will prefer putting friendship with you on the back burner, because they now perceive you as a liability and would not like having you around their homes and husbands.

- If your husband is bent on destroying you, he might indulge in character assassination, with concocted stories that might make him look good.

- When a married woman becomes single, she becomes a ready target to everyone around her. You may be viewed as easy prey by unscrupulous men, or might be bullied. If boundaries are not drawn firmly, you will end up with problems on your hands.

- Financial hurdles will loom frighteningly before you, higher than you could have envisaged.

- Finding a house which will keep you safe from the abusive partner, may prove difficult.

- Due to your personal trauma, you may not be able to concentrate on your responsibilities in your job and may end up missing promotions and other incentives.

- Your children are only children, after all. They cannot understand why their world has been turned upside down and what they have done to deserve it. Their anger is usually against both parents, but when you are the available parent, you will have to bear the brunt of their behavioral issues.

- You were once somebody's daughter. Then, you became somebody's wife. Now, you will be faced with a complete loss of identity. Who are you and how do you introduce yourself to a society that goes by such status definitions?

- There will be mood swings. On a day when all has gone well, you will be able to see a promising future. On another day, when everything has been sour and dark, including the weather, you will find yourself being grabbed by a series of negative emotions in quick succession.

- The shock! When submerged in the horror of the abusive environment, all you looked for was relief and escape. Now that that escape is yours, you will be frightened and will begin to think, "Good grief! My marriage is breaking up! When did I think I would get afflicted by divorce?"

Such haunting, nebulous experiences and fears will loom all around you and imprison you. The good news, however, is that you can overcome them and create a brand new existence for yourself, if you reach out to a certain hidden reserve within you—your inner strength. Every human being has been given inner strength by God; you must prepare yourself emotionally, spiritually, and mentally for the terrible path you will have to walk through, after the divorce.

In such a scenario, it helps to focus on the positives of getting divorced:

1. *You regain your self-respect:* For years you wondered if you were the problem. Now you realize that you gave it your best. That is worthy of respect.

2. *You start living without fear:* While in the abusive marriage, you always lived in fear, with a constant trepidation of what might come next. You don't have to be afraid anymore, since the source of your fears has been removed.

3. When you were in the abusive situation, your circumstances took up all your attention. **Now you are freed** of that heavy burden and you can give more of yourself to your children.

4. **You discover your capacity for immense strength:** After the divorce, the very fact that you've lived through beatings and verbal abuse for so many years and have survived, will give you confidence in the strength that you never knew you had.

Let me give you a glimpse of this experience, by narrating the story of my friend, Savitha, in her own words:

My best friend was with me at the Mumbai court, and the minute the female judge said, "I now decree this marriage dissolved," and hit the gravel, there was activity in the court. My friend just hugged me tight. When I walked out of the court holding my best friend's hand, it was as if I was starting to breathe again, after 18 years of claustrophobia. We got into a taxi, heading for her home in the suburbs of Mumbai.

The bubbly effect lasted three or four days, at best. The maid had been taking care of my two children. She told me that she was leaving the job. When I asked her if she had wanted more money, she said she did not but that she was getting a better opportunity elsewhere. I was left in a mess: Where would I get a maid who was trustworthy enough to look after my children?

I interviewed many maids. Since I did not have any other option, I took the best from the bad lot and employed her, at an astronomical rate. The first few days went well; she came at 9 am and left at 6 pm. On the fourth day, when I returned home, I noticed that the children were alone. When I asked them where the maid was, they said that she had left sometime back. A quick inspection revealed that some things were missing from my home—watches, silverware, and a few other expensive items. I broke down and wept. I had had a lousy day at work, too. The director had called me in and told me that while he sympathized with my situation, the business was expanding and he was expecting increased commitment and performance on my part.

I started feeling depressed. At home, while I was trying to deal with this whole maid situation, the children started misbehaving. I spent the next few days looking for counselors. I knew I needed professional help, to deal with this sensitive situation.

It's been seven years since I got divorced. I can honestly say that the first two years of being divorced were nightmarish.

My saving grace was my counselor. No matter how horrible my day or week had been, talking to her strengthened me. I felt I wouldn't break, that I could go on. So, while the children were studying, we would be locked up in the kitchen, talking over many cups of coffee. I want to tell every woman going through similar struggles, to have a personal counselor right through the bad times.

The third and fourth years were happier years. I created our own family traditions. We had family dates, where we went out together. Now, there was no longer that fear of what was going to happen. We had regained our self-respect.

My advice to you is that you must not let the initial problems put you off. Take the bold step. Things fall into place eventually. I believe I did the right thing. I am leading a fruitful and happy life. I feel like a human being, with special worth and value, and that makes up for everything."

For Savitha, her counselor was a source of support and encouragement. Help can come in the form of a counselor, friends or relatives. Even if there is no one that you can look to, God is always ready to be your source of strength. So, be strong and arm yourself for the battle.

THE D DRAMA: HOW TO FORTIFY YOURSELF FOR COURT APPEARANCES

The first step is to find a good lawyer. Do a lot of research before choosing one. Be especially careful if you choose a male lawyer, as some of them have been known to exploit women both financially and physically. Please make sure you know the procedures properly. Cite the incidents of abuse and use your evidence to back your claim. You are legally entitled to file for your rights, like marital residence, spousal support, and maintenance for the children's upkeep. If your house was purchased during the marriage, it is marital property, and therefore, half of it belongs to you, whether your name is on the deed or not. Do not allow your lawyer to lie or exaggerate, just to gain sympathy or victory. Ensure that the lawyer sticks to the truth because the minute you lie and allow false reports into the court presentation, you cannot possibly look to God for support.

Court appearances are very trying experiences. Along with the emotional trauma of painful memories being raked up (so that you prove your case), court procedures consume a lot of time and money. Not the least of which will be the lawyer's exhorbitant fees. Your relocation to lead a separated life will upset your normal routine, and the strain on you will be enormous. It is better to educate yourself about the court proceedings, before you actually enter the court.

Can you persuade your partner to agree to a mutual divorce? If you can, the procedure is simpler for both of you, and you can handle the case with or without a lawyer, as per the particulars of the court, or a single lawyer can represent both the parties. Usually, husbands agree to this if the wives refrain from asking for maintenance. If you happen to be well off or your job gets you enough to support your children and you, consider this to avoid trauma in court.

However, if the abuser is consumed with vengeance and refuses to give you a mutual divorce, you might have to file a case against him. Use the Domestic Violence laws to strengthen your case. But, let me warn you that prosecuting an abuser is not easy. Very often, there is little or no evidence of the violence, as the acts of regular choking and slapping do not leave any evidence behind.

Even if the brute has been battering the wife for years and may have violated every strand of decency between them, the court does not consider the length of time. The case rests on a one-time assault report, from a hospital or police station. Most of the time, there will be no witnesses, as the abuse is usually carried out in secrecy and in isolation.

In his seminal essay, Lundy Bancroft [12] summarizes:

"The problem is some therapists, marriage counselors, mediators, lawyers, police officers, and judges are sometimes themselves abusers. Many things work against the victim facing the justice system as abuse is such a horrid phenomenon that society often chooses to ignore it. The real abusers use the right words and sway the evaluator's judgment. The batterer can adopt the role of a hurt, sensitive man who doesn't understand how things got so bad and just wants to work it all out for the good of the family and children. The abuser with years of practice in manipulation and lies may even cry and use language that demonstrates considerable insight into his feelings. He is likely to be skilled at explaining how other people have turned the victim against him, and how she is denying him access to the children as a form of revenge. He inevitably accuses her of having mental health problems, affairs and may even state that she is hysterical or promiscuous. He will often admit to some milder acts of violence, such as shoving or throwing things, in order to increase his own credibility and create the impression that the victim is exaggerating. He may discuss errors he has made in the past and emphasize the efforts he is making to change, in order to make his partner seem vindictive and unwilling to let go of the past. Because of the abuse and the trauma, the victim will often be hostile and agitated while the abuser appears friendly, articulate, and calm and the counselors/judges often fail to adequately investigate and are thus tempted to conclude that the victim is the source of the problems in the relationship."

Yes, the batterer has the ability and marked advantage of presenting himself better than the victim during the court proceedings. Due to his ability to manipulate the sympathy of custody evaluators and judges (mostly men!), the abuser usually has the edge. The woman, who has been traumatized by years of abuse, will feel vulnerable for being made to stand before dozens of strangers, in a hostile environment, and testify to the abuse. So, she is usually not as calm and composed as the abuser is. So, please be careful—excessive emotional outbursts will not win you your case. In fact, it may make the other men present, including the judge, empathize with the husband. In fact, I have seen men intimidating their children, regarding the statements they make in court. So, sadly, at the end of it all, many victims lose their case and the batterer wins custody over the children. Hence, I say that, in spite of the trauma you have faced, you should be calm and composed in court, as this is not the time to give way to your emotions. You must work out a strategy that works well for your children and you, to avoid any more pain than absolutely necessary.

Due to such dismal reality of court proceedings, I suggest that it is best to put all personal feelings aside and get an objective, mutual friend to negotiate a fair property and asset settlement. Or else the court will decide what constitutes a fair settlement. Usually, in most countries including India, a mother automatically gets custody over the children. But, if it can be proved that she is not capable of providing for the child, the custody can be granted to the father. There are also occasions when the court awards joint custody and parents are given equal responsibility in the raising of the children and of bearing the expenses. The children will then spend equal amounts of time with their separated parents. In such cases, I have counseled spouses to set aside their personal feelings and make decisions in the best interest of their children's welfare, so that the young ones are not caught in the crossfire. On an average, about half of the cases where parents have set aside their differences in matters relating to the children, have been able to make the best of a bad situation.

THE D FORTIFICATION: MANDATORY COUNSELING AND THERAPY

You are going to be affected, and your children are going to be affected, due to the ongoing conflicts in the family before, during and after the divorce. The children will be affected according to their age, available coping mechanisms, and stages of development. If the transition is very quick, the children might find it very difficult to handle it, owing to high levels of stress. The same applies to you. If the children are not encouraged to vent out their feelings to an objective party, they might carry their baggage into adulthood. The change in lifestyle in the subsequent single parent family and possible marital changes in the future (one or both the parents may remarry) will rock the child's sense of stability.

The changes caused by the divorce might spawn a fear of abandonment and rejection. The experience can be akin to the death of a parent.

Once you are sure that divorce is going to be a reality in your home, you need to start preparing your children. Along with a trusted family friend, you will need to sit with your children and discuss the situation. I suggest the presence of a friend because they can act as a buffer should things get out of hand. A child counselor will be of good help. The children should be assured of confidentiality regarding what they share with the counselor. The counselor can prepare the children for the divorce, while you are busy preparing evidence. That will be one task off your hands. Try to discuss all your fears and their fears about the future course of action with the children, so that your children are aware of what's going on. Be sensitive to how much they can handle at any given time. The one thing that will bring you and your children closer together is a lot of love and a certain amount of transparency.

If you have not been counseled before the decision, you will definitely need it once you have settled on divorce as the only alternative. Make it a point to go at least once a fortnight, to a counselor who has specialized in counseling victims of abuse. This will prevent you from getting hurt further and will prepare you for the emotional hardships that divorce can bring. If the counselor can emphasize peace, forgiveness and God's grace, it will draw much of the emotional poison out of your system. The counselor will act as a sounding board and will help you sort through your thoughts, without judging or giving you advice.

LIFE AFTER DIVORCE: A BRAND NEW CHAPTER

Divorce is not the end of the world; it is the beginning of a new life, untainted by abuse. You will need to reinvent yourself. Nowadays, professional help and support is available, to equip you to make the change, though there are many women who have been able to do it with the help of God. Join a support group, or if you don't know of any, start one yourself, where you and other women like you can explore alternatives in lifestyle and discuss life goals in an atmosphere of respect, safety, and empathy. Such meetings

> DIVORCE IS NOT THE END OF THE WORLD; IT IS THE BEGINNING OF A NEW LIFE, UNTAINTED BY ABUSE

will rekindle resilience, strength, and creativity. Your life does not need to be limited, just because you are divorced. Believe me when I say that things won't always feel as bad as they do while at this crossroad. Life will take on a new meaning and once again, you will look forward to the future with anticipation and excitement.

To end something usually means to begin something else. In computer jargon, they call it "rebooting."

CHAPTER SIX

Rebooting

"Although the world is full of suffering, it's full also of the overcoming it."

— *Helen Keller*

You have tried everything, but a temporary separation like a soft reboot did not save your marriage. So, you went to court and chose the only option that would save your sanity. However, the truth is that divorce is a bit like a hard shutdown of a marriage. How are you supposed to reboot life thereafter?

There will be good days and there will be bad days. It is not possible to diminish or trivialize either. The important thing is that life has given you a second chance and you need to do whatever it takes to see that nothing and no one is allowed to mess it up. There are ways to build up emotional and spiritual power as you are sketching life's new blueprint.

It's borrowed.

The word in the title of this chapter is usually part of computer vocabulary. It refers to the process by which a running computer system is restarted. Rebooting can either be hard rebooting (when the power to the system is physically turned off and back on again, causing an initial boot of the machine) or soft rebooting (where the system restarts without interrupting the power). Computers are not designed for hard shutdowns, and multiple hard shutdowns can mess up the operating system.

The truth is that divorce is like a hard shutdown of a marriage, chosen as the final option to save life and sanity, when temporary separation (like a soft reboot) has not saved the marriage. No one ever gets married with the possibility of divorce in mind. But, in spite of the repercussions that follow a divorce, sometimes one is left with no option but to choose that. In such cases, the question then is: how does a person reboot life thereafter?

As seen in the previous chapter, journeying through the after-effects of divorce was much like the time that needs to be spent in a post-operative ward of a hospital, after a major surgery. Rebooting life after divorce is akin to constructing a building. It requires a similar blueprint, detailing the specifics step by step and phase by phase. Without such estimation, one could drift into chaos. Each has to make their own blueprint to solve particular issues related to their children and the problems associated with loneliness.

Divorce has to be treated like a kind of death and therefore, must be grieved. Many succumb to the pain of trying to repress it. While in an abusive marriage, disappointment was often punctuated with bouts of hope after every episode of abuse, like a roller coaster ride. Now, the marriage has come to a screeching halt.

Since pain and struggle are private, friends and relatives are unable to share the pain, as most of them cannot even fathom the extent of the loss. Some offer advice, others quick solutions and action plans, but no one is able to provide the life that one desperately craves for. Living with the dark shadows of the past keeps one from living well. Some try to remove their pain after the divorce through distraction and control. Rather than grieving and dealing with their pain, they avoid it by using drugs or alcohol, or by controlling the lives of others and dictating their actions and choices, under the guise of "doing what's best for them." Some women start relationships with emotionally unbalanced and unavailable men.

However, a few come out of this situation beautifully, by refusing to give into the negative feelings, and working through the process proactively. These women view divorce, not only as an ending but also as a new beginning, and they are able to lead rich and rewarding lives. They discover that their lives are precious and make positive choices to ensure that they have a better future.

I am presenting a few things that every newly divorced woman must carefully consider: her emotional well being, her financial security, her children, and her future relationships.

DEALING WITH EMOTIONAL OBSTACLES

Before learning how to deal with the pain, let us discuss some of the emotions a divorcee faces, so that an adequate coping mechanism can be chosen.

Fear and Uncertainty: Victims who have gone through severe abuse will experience fear and terror even after many years of having left the abusive environment. The threats of the abuser to maim or kill them, or assassinate their character, will continue to loom large. Most of the women will be filled with uncertainties, as to who will help and support them or whether they will be able to successfully juggle both a job and children.

Anger and Vengeance: Some will feel fierce anger towards themselves, their abuser, and also the callous and insensitive world outside. Some may feel, "Everybody else's life seems to be going smoothly. My life is a mess. Nothing seems to be working out for me. God must be punishing me." Few may plot out devious schemes to get hold of the abuser's possessions and work on ways to throw the abuser in jail. Vengeance drives their anger, as they are mainly consumed in hurting their abusers. They constantly engage in character assassination and create dramatic scenes with the abuser's parents or relatives. As anger begets anger, this method of dealing with pain only increases the pain.

Isolation and Loneliness: The deadliest emotions are isolation and loneliness. Scientists have found that infants denied physical contact fall sick and die. Divorce brings with it loneliness and the loss of the dream of a warm, happy family. Most divorcees isolate themselves from normal social interactions as they find it difficult to be a single person in a family-oriented world. They might also prefer to stay at home, than socialize and be the subject of gossip, judgment or pity. Many suffer with a deep unquenchable hunger of being something for someone. Mother Teresa said it well: "The most terrible poverty is loneliness, and the feeling of being unloved."

Abandonment and Bitterness: When the evil faced by a victim is so mind-numbing and the things that she has lost are irreplaceable, she may feel abandoned by everyone, including God. Many feel the bitter pang of resentment and end up completely withdrawing from the outside world, as they witness the inhumanity around them and their dreams of a happy life falls apart. They may resent God's silence, resonating with Elie Wiesel [13], a Jewish prisoner in the German concentration camp Auschwitz during World War II who expressed his anger at God, for ignoring the cries of those who called to Him for protection:

NEVER SHALL I FORGET THAT NOCTURNAL SILENCE WHICH DEPRIVED ME, FOR ALL ETERNITY, OF THE DESIRE TO LIVE

"Never shall I forget that night, the first night in camp, which has turned my life into one long night, seven times cursed and seven times sealed. Never shall I forget that smoke. Never shall I forget the little faces of the children, whose bodies I saw turned into wreaths of smoke beneath a silent blue sky. Never shall I forget those flames which consumed my faith forever. Never shall I forget that nocturnal silence which deprived me, for all eternity, of the desire to live. Never shall I forget those moments which murdered my God and my soul and turned my dreams to dust. Never shall I forget these things, even if I am condemned to live as long as God Himself. Never."

Long time exposure to emotional obstacles, which have

not been dealt with, can lead to either Post Traumatic Stress Disorder (PTSD) or Depression.

Post-Traumatic Stress Disorder: Post-Traumatic Stress Disorder (PTSD) can develop in any situation where a person feels extreme fear, horror or helplessness—military combat, serious accidents, witnessing violent deaths, etc. Some symptoms of PTSD are reacting fearfully to startling events, with extreme responses such as heart palpitations, rapid breathing, profuse sweating and imagining something terrible is going to happen though there is no danger. Many victims who have survived an abusive or violent relationship, experience PTSD due to the extreme violence and horror they have undergone. They find it very difficult to get rid of the horrible memories of the abuse, even after many years. Their painful memories haunt them every day and they spend many sleepless nights, with various nightmares replaying over and over in their heads. A poem written by Laura Lynne Navarro-Duncan portrays what this feels like:

> "**They are the memories of the past**
> They are the screaming frightening reality
> Of what I lived through
> They are the black eyes, bruised faces
> Open wounds, violations that were part of
> Everyday life
> They are far and distant memories
> That somehow get triggered and come to life
> They are the worst fears because I have lived
> Through the real nightmare
> I say my prayers and hope for another night
> The monsters stay under the bed."

PTSD can be healed when the victim becomes aware of her emotional condition and gets professional help.

Depression: Due to the traumatic experience and PTSD, many victims end up with major depression. Depression is a psychiatric disorder marked by sadness, inactivity, difficulty in thinking and concentration, loss of appetite or sleep, feelings of hopelessness and impending doom, loss of energy and interest in daily activities, anger or irritability, unexplained aches and pains, strong feelings of worthlessness or guilt and, sometimes, suicidal thoughts. Many women have shared that the depression they encounter is very heavy, dark, oppressive and completely debilitating. They sob, cry and do not get out of bed for days. When these feelings last for long periods of time—two weeks to six months—it interferes with a person's ability to work, study, eat and sleep.

The memories of the traumatic experiences one had gone through are one of the most powerful triggers of depression, and when combined with Premenstrual Dysphoric Disorder (PMDD) and Perimenopausal Depression, it can become deadly. PMDD is the repeating transitory cyclic disorder that begins in the later phase of the menstrual cycle (after ovulation) and ends shortly after menstruation begins. Perimenopausal Depression occurs in victims aged between 45 and 55 years, who have been in abused marriages for long periods. The suicidal talk of such a person should be taken seriously and people close to them should be able to identify symptoms like a sudden switch from being extremely depressed to acting calm and happy, expressing strong feelings of hopelessness, or calling/visiting people to say goodbye and giving away prized possessions.

EMOTIONAL HEALTH

As there is a lot of stigma attached to mental health issues, many hide it and, to alleviate or numb the pain, self-medicate with alcohol, nicotine, illicit drugs, food, work, shopping, television, sex, pornography, internet surfing, gambling, withdrawal, self-hypnosis and meditation. However, such control techniques usually work only in the short-term, and result in the issue being evaded rather than being dealt with. Following are some of the more common methods of healing, used by people with Depression or PTSD.

Medical Solutions: One possible solution for Depression are antidepressants called SSRIs (serotonin reuptake inhibitors) that raise the levels of neurotransmitters, mainly serotonin, in the brain, thus elevating the mood from a depressed state to a more normal state of mind. Some doctors recommend antidepressant medication in combination with hormone replacement therapy (usually estrogen plus progesterone, or occasionally estrogen alone). A mood stabilizer is given in addition to antidepressant therapy in some cases.In cases of severe depression, medication is combined with psychotherapy.

The primary treatment for PTSD is psychotherapy, to increase a sense of control over life, often including medication. Combining medication and psychotherapy can assist in improving skills and coping mechanisms to address the symptoms, and help one to feel better about oneself.

Two types of psychotherapy are highly recommended for PTSD and Depression: Interpersonal Therapy and Cognitive Behavioral Therapy (CBT). Interpersonal Therapy focuses on understanding how changing human relationships may contribute to, or relieve, depression. CBT is a psychotherapeutic treatment that helps patients to understand the thoughts and feelings that influence behaviors, and focuses on changing what they think (cognitive) and what they do (behavior), thus increasing desired behaviors even if the situation does not change. During the course of the treatment, people learn how to identify and change destructive or disturbing thought patterns that have a negative influence on behavior, such that they can take control of how they interpret and deal with things even in aspects of the world that are beyond their control.

However, for CBT to be effective, the individual must be willing to spend time and effort analyzing her thoughts and feelings. This form of therapy calls for recalling traumatic events at length and in great detail, which some individuals with severe mental trauma may find very unpleasant. As depression normally relapses, many patients are addicted to antidepressants and such medications become a way of life. Mood stabilizers, when taken in high doses, can cause hand tremors and difficulty with fine/detailed tactile functioning like fastening a chain. Some medicines cause dry mouth, slight tremors, faster heartbeats, constipation, sleepiness, weight gain and anxieties. Some of the more serious side effects are problems with urination, forgetfulness, falls, confusions and dangerously high blood pressure.

NATURAL SOLUTIONS

Some natural solutions are changes in lifestyle that include exercise, meditation, eating healthy foods, good sleep and engaging in new and interesting activities. Omega 3 (fish or flax) and EPA/DHA oils can sometimes enhance one's mood; two to three capsules with each meal may alleviate depression and improve cognitive function. Hypericum, or St John's Wort, is said to be as effective as antidepressants in cases of mild depression, although there is little published evidence for its effectiveness in moderate to severe depression. A good source of Complementary & Alternative Medicine (CAM) for Mental Health information can be found at *http://mentalhealthamerica.net/sites/default/files/MHA_CAM. pdf.* Further, building skills to manage stress and balance emotions improve a person's ability to cope and bounce back from adversity, trauma, and loss. In other words, learning how to recognize and express emotions can make a person more resilient. In most cases, the best approach involves a combination of social support—from friends and family who understand the situation—lifestyle changes, emotional skill building, managing stress, practising relaxation techniques and channeling negative thought patterns.

SELF-HELP BOOKS AND COUNSELING

Self-help books can also be a productive source of help. Viktor Frankl, a Jewish psychotherapist, who survived the Auschwitz concentration camp, lays out the vital importance of having a purpose to live for and the ability to find meaning in life in the harshest of circumstances, in his book, *"Man's Search for Meaning." "Seven Habits of Highly Effective People"* by Stephen Covey explains the theory behind a purpose driven life and provides the tools to help put it into practice. *"The Language of Letting Go"* by Melody Beattie, *"Turn My Mourning into Dancing"* by Henri Nouwen and *"The Power of Now"* by Eckhart Tolle are some inspirational books for those who want to cultivate the right attitude. *"Women who Love Too Much"* by Robin Norwood and *"How to Sleep Alone in a King Size Bed"* by Theo Pauline Nestor can help divorced / single women with guidance on relationships, and might keep them from getting entangled with emotionally unbalanced men.

But honestly, if you ask my opinion, I have not got much benefit out of these self-help books.

WORLDVIEW AND HEALING

It is true that a person's philosophy has far-reaching repercussions when domestic abuse is in the mix. If the abused does not have a solid worldview in place, they can easily get carried away by the torrent of their negative emotions. A good worldview helps in dealing with the emotional wounds and the low self-esteem, and in working through painful memories.

A worldview is the harmony of a person's beliefs about the world and it is the lens through which one views, evaluates and understands reality. It defines God, our origin, our destiny, life, death, values, morals, goals and relationships. Our worldview is shaped by our parents, the society and culture we belong to, our friends, the books we read and so on. Though it impacts many areas of our lives, like our decisions and attitudes, many of us have never questioned our belief systems and have never analyzed whether it is harmful or accurate.

Most of the questions that hammer a victim's mind are along the lines of "Why should such an evil thing like this happen to me?" and "Where is God when I am hurting?" Sorting out these issues will help the victim regain stability when moving forward. A healthy worldview is one which should be able to answer in a coherent and consistent manner the four fundamental questions of life—how did I come into existence? (Origin), Why am I here? (Meaning), Why do bad things happen to good people? (Morality), and Where will I go after I die? (Destiny). For the severely wounded and crippled victim, who has the terrible feeling that she is falling into a bottomless pit, developing reckless confidence in a source of strength higher than herself is of utmost importance, in order to move ahead.

I would like to present to you the story of my neighbor Ramya, who had tried everything on earth to come out of depression.

I begged and pleaded with my parents to let me work after completing my studies. But they were adamant that I get married. They found a smart, well-educated, and well-settled groom for me. However good that sounded, I still wanted to work for a few years and stand on my own two feet. They cajoled and coaxed me and said that I could work after I got married: "The groom we have in mind is an understanding and caring man, who wouldn't have any problem if you went back to work," they said. I still wasn't convinced but I went ahead with the marriage, as I absolutely loved my parents, especially my father. He's been the best father ever and I wanted to please him. So in a few months, I married to the "smart, well-educated and well-settled groom".

I remember being a bit shy on my wedding night. But my husband didn't seem so shy; he treated the wedding bed as a confessional. He started telling me about all his previous relationships with many women. I was mortified and disgusted. I suddenly felt very scared and began hoping I wouldn't get any sexual transmitted diseases. I hadn't even had a boyfriend and here my parents had married me to someone who seemed to be a seasoned lover. That night passed without much ado.

The next few months were horrible as my husband had a temper. Every discussion would end in arguing and bickering, and this went on for months. What really irritated me was that, in front of my parents my husband was the best husband ever. I knew it was a big act but my parents were so happy; my father would keep telling me how lucky I was and asking wasn't it good that I had listened to him. My father was so happy and proud of my husband that I just didn't know how to tell him that these last four months had been so terrible. So, I just hugged and thanked him.

Then I received the bad news that my husband had got a job transfer and that we were moving to another city. I was so crestfallen. The thought of leaving my parents behind and going someplace alone with my husband scared me. I don't know why but to stay with my husband all alone in a new city terrified me.

A few months after we moved, I discovered that I was pregnant. I was so excited when I told my husband. He just looked at me blankly. He didn't seem happy at all. He stopped talking to me after that. We were like strangers in the same house. This went on for months. Not only was he withdrawn but he refused to give me money to run the house. He insisted that I work. I explained that I was five months pregnant and that nobody would give me a job, but he just wouldn't listen. I had to sell most of my jewellery to run the house and to pay for my scans and other tests.

My mother had wanted to come and be with me during my confinement but my husband refused. We had a big fight and, for the first time in our marriage, he hit me. Not once but a few times. I was stunned. No one had ever hit me before. Not my parents, not my teachers. I protested and he hit me harder and, this time, he had a number of choice words for me. He told me that he hated the sight of me. We started sleeping in separate rooms but every day he would abuse me and say nasty things to me. I felt so alone. I hadn't made a single friend in this city. So, there was no one to share my sadness with. I cried everyday but didn't want my unborn baby to sense my sadness, so I tried to be happy. No matter how mad I was with my husband, I still cooked and cleaned the house. Since I had no money to pay a maid, I had to do the work myself. Right till my 9th month, I struggled to cook and clean.

My beautiful daughter, Tanya, was born healthy and she was beautiful. That didn't change my husband's attitude. He was more distant than ever. He didn't spend any time with the baby. I felt depressed. How could he not love such a precious and adorable baby? My limited funds had almost run out. I pleaded with my husband to give me money for the baby. He had such a big job. He gave me a pittance. I had spent every rupee on the baby. I couldn't remember the last time I had bought something nice for myself.

My parents came to see us after a month. They couldn't come earlier as my mother wasn't well. I was so overjoyed to see them and couldn't stop crying. Once again, my husband put on an award-winning show. My parents bought it. I had enough of this charade and I was ready to end it, but my mother looked so pale and sickly. What if something happened to her? I decided to just keep quiet. They left and, once again, I was stuck with a husband who didn't care for his daughter or his wife. Almost once a week, I would get severely beaten up for no reason. His words were very cruel. I ended up in severe depression and had to take antidepressants for a while.

We went for our first family holiday when Tanya was four. When we came back a month later, I discovered I was pregnant again. I couldn't believe it. Nothing had changed between my husband and me. When I told him, he reacted the same way as before. This time, I didn't want to keep my mother away. My husband shouted at me and hit me, but I still phoned her and called her to be with me. My husband's "good husband" act didn't last for more than four days. After four days of pasted smiles, he showed his true self. He started abusing me. He slapped me a few times but made sure that he did this when my mother was out.

One day, when my mother was sleeping, we had the biggest fight ever, and while we were fighting, my mother came out. We both hadn't noticed her. My husband slapped me and pushed me. I fell. My mother came running to catch me. She was screaming and shouting. I'd never seen my mother so angry. She started yelling at my husband. He abused her and said horrible things to her and about both my parents. My mother was shocked. We went into the guest room. She asked me how long this had been going on. I told her the truth. She broke down and called my father.

They spoke for a long time on the phone. Two days later, my father came home. I told my parents everything. My father kept apologizing. He begged me to forgive him and asked me to pack up and come with them. I did as they said because I didn't want to *take any more abuse. I was six months pregnant then.*

Timothy was born a few months later. My husband never called. He didn't miss me or my children. I called my husband to tell him. He was as distant as ever. "Absence makes the heart grow fonder"—who wrote this crummy quote?

My depression relapsed and I had to take antidepressants again. I read a lot of self-help books and I recited some of the quotes to myself:"When things go wrong, when the road is uphill, when life is full of twists and turns, never quit as success is failure turned inside out." But it did not help me much as I was desperate and could not stick to the fight. Though the principles and concepts were good and may have worked for many, it did not help me, as I lacked the will power at this juncture to implement them.

My parents really helped me during this time. My father got a job as a consultant. It broke my heart to see him go back to work but we couldn't manage financially. I took over some of the household chores from my mother. A small part of me hoped that my husband missed me and would come begging for me to return to him, with the children. That never happened. After a year of separation, my counselor told me to start divorce proceedings. I refused. Since he was earning so well, I insisted that we start with child support. That was a big mistake. Four years have passed and the child support case is still going on. I should have just got a divorce and moved on. But that will come next.

My parents have been amazing. I know they've put their life on hold for us. My parents had saved some money and had wanted to travel and see the world. They've spent everything on us. I hope I can make it up to them one day. My husband has no interest in the children and they are too young to understand what is happening. We've made a life for ourselves and I know I wouldn't have been able to make it without my parents' support.

STEPS TO COMPLETE EMOTIONAL HEALING

Emotional healing takes time. It is a very clichéd notion, but true nonetheless. If you are weary of living with painful memories and of trying to work through the ache in your heart with counseling, self-help books or medication, be courageous! There is hope.

I have outlined a few proactive ways in which you can help the healing process along, with the help of God. I suggest that you take a notebook and a pen for this exercise and write down a little prayer, asking God to assist you in this process.

EMOTIONAL HEALING TAKES TIME. IT IS A VERY CLICHÉD NOTION, BUT TRUE NONETHELESS

Make notes: Jot down every incident of violence and abuse that you have faced during your relationship. As you remember every episode of violence—the name calling, the beatings, the bullying, the taunting, the mocking—you will start to feel a deep pain rise within you.

Cry: Don't push this pain down. Allow the pain to reach the surface. Let the tears flow. If you feel like weeping and sobbing, do it. Don't deny your feelings, as denial may give rise to numbness, shock and an inability to carry out your daily routines.

Learning to accept: After having made notes of all your past episodes of abuse and having cried over them, you will reach the stage of acceptance. Once you have accepted all that has happened to you, it will be easier to move on with your life. Acceptance will enable you to declare all the right statements, like: "Okay! So I would never have wanted it but it did happen to me. What I want to do now is to get out of the debris of divorce with dignity and sanity intact".

Just let it go: At this stage, you have to make a decision to let go of the past. Whenever the memory of the past begins to surface, you must refuse to indulge them. DON'T GO THERE. Tell yourself, "I will not go there," and think of something else. You need to make place in your life for peace and strength. Letting go is very hard. Healing will take time and cannot happen overnight, but it will eventually get easier.

Forgive, forgive, and forgive: Try to relinquish your pain by forgiving. Forgiveness is not about your abuser but it is about you. Unless you let go, you cannot make room for a new life. Lack of forgiveness will lead to bitterness. Bitterness will take root in your emotional being and will paralyze your ability to feel.

Tap into your faith: There can be no faith without trust and no trust without faith. Your faith will hold you in good stead, if you hold onto it firmly. If you get some bad news, or something untoward happens, without rushing into panic, immediately say, "God is in control. He is responsible for whatever happens to me so why should I worry."

Replace: When you switch on the light, you switch off the darkness. In the same way, you have to replace whatever you are expelling from your life with the opposite: replace hatred with love; sickness with good health; suspicion with trust; fear with confidence; despair with hope; sadness with joy, etc. Remember, "As you think, so shall you be" (Proverbs 23:7, in the Bible). Choose to focus on what is positive in your life.

DEALING WITH FINANCES

I am no financial expert but the fact remains that after a divorce, no matter what the court verdict is, you will need to sort through your financial situation and come up with a long term plan that is independent of the alimony or child support, if any. Most women usually do not have anything to do with finances in their homes. If that was the case, it is no longer a good idea to stay ignorant. Staying dependent on court-awarded money is never a good idea because it is not something that is guaranteed long-term.

Get a job, if you are not already working. See if you can do a few short-term courses to get yourself more up-to-date, before you go job hunting. Learning how to take control of your money starts with a budget, and hence learn how to create a budget that fits well with your lifestyle. To make a budget, gather every financial statement that includes any information regarding a source of income or expense. Record all your sources of income and your estimated expenses, both fixed and variable, that you might incur over the period of a month. Fixed expenses are those that stay relatively the same every month and variable expenses are those that change significantly from month to month. Total your monthly income and monthly expense, and put these on spreadsheets. If your income and expense columns are equal, then all of your income is accounted for and has been budgeted for a specific expense. If you are in a situation where expenses are higher than income, prune possible areas in variable expenses to balance the difference. To make sure you are staying on track, review your budget every month, comparing the actual expenses versus what you had estimated while creating the budget. This will show you where you did well and where you may need to improve. Read up on finances and investments. *"The Total Money Makeover: A Proven Plan For Financial Fitness"* by Dave Ramsey is a good book that will help you get started. Get all the information you can on retirement funds and investments.

Most importantly, find someone who is divorced and who was able to sort through her finances well, and learn from her. I am sure you will be able to find at least a few people who have been able to do well in this area. Be proactive in gaining wisdom in this aspect of your life, by collecting all the information you can and applying them. Most women are not even aware of their own strengths until they are pushed over the edge. This might be a good opportunity for you to make some discoveries of your own.

DEALING WITH CHILDREN

Parents need to remember that their children are vulnerable and will need to see counselors or therapists to deal with the trauma of their parents getting divorced or with the confusion of growing up in an abusive environment. *"Problems Associated with Children's Witnessing of Domestic Violence"* by Jeff Edleson, an expert on batterer treatment programs, provides an in-depth discussion of the ways in which children's health can be affected when they are witness to domestic violence. Edleson reviews various studies reporting statistical evidence of behavioral, emotional, cognitive and long-term problems associated with children being witness to domestic violence. Research shows that 50% of men who frequently abuse their wives, also abuse their children [14]. Children may be "inadvertently" hurt as they may be hit by items thrown by the batterer, and older children, in particular, may be hurt trying to protect their mother. Regular counseling can help in the healing process of such traumatized children. Even though parents might be at loggerheads with each other, they should never poison the impressionable minds of children by saying nasty things about each other. When parents force the child to take sides, the child is put in a very difficult and uncomfortable position. Custody and visitation are difficult issues and parents need to constantly keep their children's best interests in mind.

If your ex-spouse has visitation rights, let there be another person with you when he comes to take the children for the court-allotted time. Don't worry that he may try to lie to your children about you. When talking to the children, make it a point to avoid bad-mouthing their father and explain to them why you were unable to give them a normal, two-parent family. Keep pouring love into their lives, for that will heal them more than gifts or manipulative talk. Tell them again and again that you and your ex have divorced each other. but that you still love them. If they ask you what you did wrong, don't try to get defensive or offensive in an attempt to absolve yourself and put the blame on their father. Remember that their young minds cannot handle this and it could have a serious impact on their character. Try to talk it out, and love them and be with them. Give each one of them a hug and tell them how much you love them.

WHEN CHILDREN START ACTING UP

Hatred diminishes human beings. It makes them less than who they are meant to be. I bring you Savithri's story to show you that hatred is never the answer.

My biggest problem after my divorce turned out to be my children. My teenagers were 12 and 14. They developed a full blown hatred towards me. It was terrible. I had not wanted the divorce, even though my husband had hurt me in every possible way. He fell in love with someone else and wanted out, but in spite of his less than human treatment of me, I still wanted to stay in the marriage because I knew it wasn't a safe world out there. Unfortunately, even if one person doesn't want the divorce, the person still ends up being called a divorcee. My children blamed the whole thing on me. We didn't talk much during and after the divorce. So they assumed everything was my fault. They felt that it was something I had done that drove their father away. They spoke to me with disrespect.

I found a way of helping them with their sadness. I had this Christian friend who used to talk about forgiveness. She said, "You must forgive your husband." She said that it was important to forgive him and that it was also important for the children to see that I had forgiven him. One day, while my friend and I were sitting with my daughter, my daughter told me that she hated her daddy. I must admit that I was very surprised. My children seemed to love him. But now, all the love seemed to have gone out of the window. She started weeping bitterly.

My friend explained that my husband wasn't a bad man but suffered from a "Serious Character Disorder." Such people see themselves as the center of the universe and believe that all other people were created to meet their demands. "So your father," she said, "is incapable of thinking about anyone else but himself."

I tried to reason with my daughter: "If your father had lost his leg in an accident or if he had lost his eyes or any other part of his body, or was very sick, would you stop loving him?" She said "No." I said, "So, he has this disorder and we must love him in spite of that. It was very tough for me to say this to them but it got easier while talking. I knew I had to back what I was saying, so I allowed them to meet their father often.

By showing them that I had no problems with their father, I was also helping them deal with their confusion and anger. Soon, the anger and hatred seemed to leave them.

WHEN YOU FORGET YOURSELF

My advice to you is that you must never make your children the center of your universe. Try to give importance to yourself as a human being. Real life stories emphasize this more than mere words. Revathi's story will drive this point home.

My divorce had to happen. I had absolutely no doubts, no confusion, and no second thoughts about it. My children's lives were endangered as my husband had serious mental problems, which he refused to accept. I landed in the divorce courts and my marriage was terminated. In the weeks that followed, my children and I spent hours every day talking about the situation, holding hands, crying, going through fits of anger and other turbulent emotions that usually follow a divorce. My children were angry, then sad, and then happy again. The same was true of me. I was not able to rise above my own pain and so I was also a willing partner in the screaming matches that we had. My girls, who were 18, 15, and 9, discussed this a lot amongst themselves. My motto was: "Let's move on." We had a fairly happy transition, having dealt with and having spoken openly about what we were going through. My girls were very social and were a part of a couple of youth groups. They had their friends over very often. They were good children.

In retrospect, I realize that I was wrong in making my children the center of my world. Yes, it is important to help children deal with their hurt and to be there for them. But the mistake is to ignore your own healing and not dealing with your own pain.

Fast-forward to a few years later. My daughters have married. They all married wonderful men and have happy marriages. One daughter lives in the same city and the other two moved to different cities as soon as they got married. There is no place for me in their lives. They love me no doubt, but apart from talking twice a week on the phone, they have their lives and they don't need me. I've four grandchildren but my daughters haven't asked for my help with their children. While bringing up my children, I was so busy working and looking after my girls that I didn't have time to make any friends. And now, my lack of knowledge shows when I meet with other people. I have tried making friends, but at 56, it is extremely hard. It didn't take me too long to realize that the only people who were available for any kind of social relationships were other single mothers and divorced women. We were not welcome into two-parent homes for obvious reasons.

I joined a single parent group and realized that these women were so smart. They hadn't put their lives on hold like I did but had made it a point to be socially active and aware. They had upgraded their skills, read up on all the latest technology, and seemed to be aware of everything that was going on. Their knowledge of cloud computing totally outdid my knowledge of the best fabric conditioner for delicate clothing. I felt so inadequate with them. So, I stopped going out with them.

I would like to share this with women who are considering divorce or are about to be thrown into single parenthood: yes, your children are important when you are separated or divorced, but then, so are you. Keep your identity alive. Discover yourself, make friendships that last. Don't live and breathe only for your children because when they go on to carve their own lives, you will find yourself so alone. They might visit you for a few days every year, but what about the remaining 350+ days? What are you going to do with yourself? Are you going to start planning for their next visit? I hope not. So, make a new life for yourself and do the things that you like.

Dealing With Future Relationships

After a divorce, many victims struggle with unrealistic expectations, monstrous insecurities and debilitating feelings of anxiety, loneliness and depression. A few try to reduce or anesthetize the pain and the hurt that they are going through with strong feelings that come from romance and sex. Anyone who helps them looks like their knight in shining armour. ANYONE! Then they might feel attractive and secure, and end up in a rebound or abusive relationship again.

In a rebound relationship, an empty lonely person who is still hurting from a previous broken relationship, denies the inner void and tries to get into another meaningful relationship by treating it as a substitute or replacement. The needy, vulnerable ones use this new relationship as a coping mechanism to overcome pain and to deal with negative feelings like depression or loneliness. For them, it seems more appealing to focus on a new love than to focus on healing the pain of a divorce. However, hidden feelings of sadness and loss often act as powerful undercurrents that prevent full commitment to the new relationship, making it unsatisfying. Such a rebound relationship often ends in severe hurt and suffering, and the person's situation will look like having "jumped from the frying pan into the fire." This narration by my colleague about her sister, gives us a glimpse of the dangers of rebound relationships.

"My sister acted like an obsessed idiot; no one can be blamed for what happened to her."

Let me admit right at the start that my sister got a raw deal. Firstly, she was forced by my mother into marriage with a man she had no wish to marry. Her prospective mother-in-law would come each day and tell her what a blessing she would be to her home. Finally, my parents prevailed upon my sister and she was married off to this man.

He hated her and started to beat her. They had a beautiful son, but the husband used to beat the 6-month-old child as well. Since this is about life after divorce, I don't want to dwell any more on what happened before my sister got divorced. The bottom line is that the divorce took place. My sister was free. The court was very sympathetic to my sister and managed to get her son good child support. The court provided good support for my sister as well.

Since my sister had bottled up the feelings of being violated, insulted and humiliated, when her current situation set her free, she turned into someone entirely different. Although she was happy, we felt that it was a kind of false bravado. I felt that when a marriage dies, one would have to give it time to heal. But my sister declared that she was healed straightaway and that the past was behind her.

She wouldn't go out much, but would spend time browsing the internet and visiting sites that arranged marriages. Within four months of her divorce, she started looking for another husband. My sister was very beautiful and she uploaded her photograph onto one of the sites. She received several replies and communicated with a few. She finally settled for this really good looking man. They started communicating regularly.

As far as my sister was concerned, she was not open to reason. This man seemed besotted by her and they met subsequently. He still hadn't revealed much about himself to her, apart from saying that he was from another city. My sister became very mysterious from there on. We knew something was going on, but she was on a high. One day, when we were having one of our close conversations, she mentioned that she was getting married again. I was shocked when I heard this. I said to her, "Don't be silly! It's hardly six months since your divorce!" But she responded saying, "I need a father for my son, and I need a companion as well. This is the man of my dreams. This time, I'm making my own choice."

Although I tried to convince her to give it more time, to learn more about this person, she remained adamant, saying, "What do we have to wait for? We don't need to wait for anything. He's had a bad marriage and so have I. We can help one another heal." He gave her this promise: he would take good care of her and her son. This is exactly what single mothers are vulnerable to, when someone shows up like a knight in shining armor, saying, "I will love your son like he was my own." You tend to lose all reason and all caution gets thrown to the wind. My sister became totally obsessed with this person. She started acting like an obsessed idiot. She was not even ready to discuss this and was not ready to meet with the elders, like my aunts and uncles.

Just a day before he was scheduled to meet our parents and a week before they were to be married, she got an email from him saying, "I'm so sorry! Please forgive me if you can. I'm marrying a doctor tomorrow." Apparently, he'd been trying out three women, including my sister, that he had met online and had wanted to pick the one who fitted his plans the best. He must have met with all three as well. At that point, my sister did not have much information about this man— where he lived, what he did for a living— knowing only that he had referred vaguely to some business. I'm not sure if that man was being truthful to my sister or if he was just making all this up.

My sister had not gone through the normal process of a divorce—the grieving, the denial, the anger, the acceptance and the healing. She had not gone through any of these phases. She just rushed through and, in being rejected so badly, she committed suicide. My nephew called us one day and said, "Thai, please come. Mummy's not getting up." She'd taken an overdose of sleeping pills, just a few days after she had received the mail from that man. I know it's a terrible story, but I'm sharing it because I don't want the same thing that happened to my sister to happen to others.

I want to tell all single mothers and divorced women who've gotten out of abusive marriages: please don't get married immediately. It takes two years for feelings to stabilize and for healing to take place. If you get married within two years, it might turn out to be a bigger disaster and you may end up marrying *someone who is a bigger brute than your ex-husband. Ladies, please be careful. I don't want what happened to my sister to happen to any of you.*

Beloved, such disasters can happen due to manipulative men who use your loneliness as a chance to enter your life and use you sexually and financially. Dangerous men will start a friendship with an agenda in mind and they will want instant commitment and intimacy. Such men may have a hidden life; they may be violent, mentally ill, emotionally unavailable or may have issues with addictions. Look out for the warning signs of abusive men.

Realize that you have survived the abuse. Relax and take a hard look at yourself. Make decisions about how you are going to spend your time. When you do that, new interests and hobbies are frequently discovered and you don't need someone else's presence to keep you happy. Enjoy your single status. Listen to your God-given instincts and choose your friendships carefully. Never discuss your personal matters with any new friends or acquaintances. Remarriage can give plenty of hope, lots of love and a desire to construct some form of joint life; but it has its own challenges, that make it a little more tenuous than the first marriage. According to an article in Psychology Today [15], "an astonishing 75% of the broken-hearted get married all over again. And if you count among the remarried those who merge lives and households without legal ratification, the de facto remarriage rate is even higher. Yet a whopping 60% of remarriages fail. And they do so even more quickly; after an average of 10 years, 37% of remarriages have dissolved versus 30% of first marriages ... three decades of a persistently high divorce rate have encouraged couples to test the waters by living together before marrying. But this actually dims the likelihood of marital success." The article also says that since each partner will have his or her various links to the past, they need to allow enough time for the cognitive and emotional reorganization that must take place, so that the impact of the ghosts from the past is minimized. It takes time to trust again. Time is also needed to grieve the end of the previous marriage. This reduces the risk of staying covertly attached to it, because losing someone you once cared about is not a small issue. The presence of kids from the previous marriage, who themselves are in a state of mourning over the loss of an intact family, poses a great challenge. A lot of soul-searching has to be done and one of the keys to success in remarriage is that the couples have to be less selfish and understand that there is a history that needs to be worked out. They also need to nourish the relationship on a daily basis, refraining from things that threaten the marriage.

Life will always throw obstacles our way. Especially ones that we had never imagined we would have to face. It is what you do with these bad experiences that will determine your destiny. Can delight be found in debris? Can beauty be found in ashes? It is possible. Here are the inspiring anthems of a few women who overcame abuse and have come out thriving.

CHAPTER SEVEN

Inspiring Anthems

"To keep our faces toward change and behave like free spirits in the presence of fate is strength undefeatable."

— Helen Keller

There are always those who lack understanding and pass judgments on women from broken marriages. Society, at large, is none too sensitive. How does one thrive and not just survive after a broken marriage?

The media-generated image of the lonely and financially strapped divorcee is a stereotype that needs to be shattered. As a counter to it, consider these three women, varying in age, race, and predicament, who have thrived after initiating their own abuse-related divorces. Their intense fears of financial, emotional and romantic ruin never materialized; on the contrary, their lives improved immeasurably and their self-esteem soared!

The torturous question is: *how?*

So far, the physical, psychological, spiritual and emotional aspects of abuse-related trauma have been discussed. However, at the end of it all, emotions need to concretize themselves into decisions.

There are always those who lack understanding and pass judgments on women from broken marriages. Society, at large, is none too sensitive. The future looms large in the distance. How does one thrive and not just survive after a broken marriage?

To show you that life can be abundantly full, even after unexpected detours, here are three true life stories of women from different countries (including India), who share the details of how they did it.

Leslie Morgan Steiner: *"Instead of asking an abused wife why she stays with a man who beats her, have the empathy and courage to help her on her way."*

You would never have guessed Leslie's secret if you had met her at a friend's child's birthday party, in the hallway at work, or at a neighbor's barbecue. As a young woman, she had fallen in love with and married a man who beat her regularly and who very nearly killed her. "I don't look the part," she declares. "I have an MBA and an undergraduate degree from an Ivy League school. I live in a red brick house on a tree-lined street in one of the prettiest neighborhoods in Washington, DC. I've got 15 years of marketing experience at a Fortune 500 company and a best-selling book about motherhood to my name."

The most important thing today, after her second marriage, is that she has a smart, loyal husband with a sexy gap in his front teeth; a real softie, who puts out food for the stray kittens, in the alley near their home. They have three spirited children, not to mention a dog and three cats. I love the way Leslie tells her story, without any bitterness or a need to paint her abuser black: "Few people will understand what torture it is to fall in love with a good man who cannot leave a violent past behind." She had met the warm and loving Conor on the subway. He was handsome, street-smart and had a great sense of humor, which made the whole thing look like they were a made for each other. The harrowing reality of his abusive nature became evident even before they were married. A couple of days before the wedding, he grabbed her neck with the serious intention of killing her. She forgave him because all the arrangements were made, not to mention the fact that she was desperately in love with him. By then, Conor had shared with her that he'd been abused regularly since he was a boy, and he couldn't figure out why love and rage danced so intimately together in his psyche. So, she went ahead with the fairy-tale wedding, at which the entire staff of *Seventeen* magazine (where she held a glamorous job) turned up.

It wasn't long after their idyllic honeymoon that Leslie discovered she had made a mistake that many others like her have made: she had fallen in love with the wrong person. At first, she tried to ignore the fights they began to have over just about anything. "Maybe that's the way it is in all marriages," she reassured herself. But, that was only until the violence began: he pushed her down the stairs of the house they bought together; poured coffee grinds over her hair as she dressed for a critical job interview; choked her during an argument; and threatened her with a gun. Several times, he came close to making good on his threat to kill her.

IT WASN'T LONG AFTER THEIR IDYLLIC HONEYMOON THAT LESLIE DISCOVERED SHE HAD MADE A MISTAKE THAT MANY OTHERS LIKE HER HAVE MADE

With each attack, Leslie lost another piece of herself. For many years, Leslie concealed the dark secret from everybody. Despite the severe battering, Leslie stayed on because she loved him and, after every episode, he would cry in a pathetic way and promise to change. He never did and it was only when she met a sympathetic and wise friend (who later became her husband) that she realized she had the right to safety and a better life. No wonder she says, "Instead of asking an abused wife why stay with a man who beats her, have the empathy and courage to help her on her way."

She went through with the divorce, which she had dreaded to think about earlier. She has become a successful editor. To inspire other women to walk out of abusive marriages, she has written a book called *"Crazy Love,"* which is all about her abusive marriage. She has also edited *"Mommy Wars: Stay-at-Home and Career Moms Face Off on Their Choices, Their Lives, Their Families,"* a collection of essays by women struggling to balance motherhood and their careers. After her divorce, she received an MBA in Marketing from Wharton School of Business and worked in Marketing for Johnson & Johnson, before transitioning into writing, as the General Manager of the magazine, Washington Post. She has just released her third book as an author, on the effect of fertility treatments in modern motherhood.

Sheeba Thomas: *"I couldn't believe this was my reality. And I couldn't see a way out."*

I didn't understand my situation. How could I experience domestic violence and abuse when mine was a Christian home? My husband and I were born again Christians. It would shock all who hear this but abuse has never restricted itself to any one religious persuasion, socio-economic strata or educational background.

The abuse had started subtly and grown insidiously. Nobody who knew my husband or me would have imagined the situation at our home. We had both been Pastors' kids. I had never been rebellious; had graduated from college with Honors in Psychology; played the keyboard like an angel; and was a leader in the church youth group. I had a relationship with Jesus but I must confess that it was more or less superficial. I met Reji at Bible College and was drawn to the fact that he was an expert in theology and doctrine, and seemed to genuinely care about people's salvation. We got married and the church was filled with pastors from all around India, who prayed blessings over us. It was an elaborate, God-centered event.

The problems began after we returned from our honeymoon and moved into our new home. Imagine this: he used up the entire cupboard in our bedroom for his stuff and told me to use the cupboard in the guest room. I was earning a substantial amount of money from giving music lessons and he insisted that it would be best if he took charge of the household funds. I had to beg him for money when I needed to buy personal things. He was controlling and constantly monitored what I spent. Once, when I bought some things for the showcase in the hall, he blew up because I had not discussed it with him first. I had no say in the décor of our home; he did it all up according to his liking, which was far from mine. I had to get his permission to even put a picture up on the wall!

Gradually, I noticed that my husband had anger management issues. His temper was always simmering just below the surface. While it is true that he never ever struck me, he did often push me aside roughly, and once, shook me so violently that I felt my bones rattle. I lived in perpetual fear, always trying to avoid things that would set him off. Nothing I said or did ever pleased him. I did not share what I was going through with anyone, as I knew it would break my parents' heart. Also, lack of love and communication hardly seemed like serious marital problems, when there were other women getting battered and raped by their husbands. Only those who have been stifled, suffocated and oppressed the way I was, know the desperation it brews. I thought things would improve after I got pregnant but they did not. God was so gracious in blessing us with a robust baby boy. However, even young Matthew could not bring joy into Reji's life. It was not long before Matthew's sunny temperament got snuffed out slowly, in response to the oppressive atmosphere at home. For Matthew and me, it was like walking on egg shells every day.

One night, when I had angered Reji by dropping a plate that slipped from my hand and broke, he ran towards me in sheer fury. I put my hands, instinctively shielding my face, because I thought he was going to hit me. The gesture angered him even more and he grabbed my shoulders, shook me violently, and shoved me into Matthew's room, where I fell on the floor. It was around the time of night when Matthew is fast asleep. So I was taken aback when I heard him ask, "Mummy, did Papa do this to you? Why is he so angry?" I simply climbed into his bed and held him close, as we both cried softly. I slept there that night, too fearful to return to the master bedroom and be with Reji.

By the next morning, I had made my decision. I went to meet the chief pastor and broke down, as I shared with him all that I had been through, during the seven years of my marriage. He was shocked and surprised because I had never said a word to anyone before. He sent for Reji that night and spoke with us. Reji did not deny his bouts of anger but blamed me for provoking him, by my "lack of finesse" and because of my "not being submissive enough." I did not argue, as my heart was heavy.

This went on for 18 months; we went for regular counseling sessions but nothing changed. The counselor put Reji under an "accountability elder," someone he was supposed to call up whenever he felt a rage attack coming on. When I saw Matthew turning into a timid and withdrawn child, I knew I had to make some serious decisions. I did not want to cause a ripple in the church by speaking of divorce, so I quietly separated from Reji. Though deeply grieved, my parents insisted that Matthew and I stay with them. We did, and with their love and prayers, some semblance of joy filtered into our lives.

The one thing that I was sure of was that I never wanted to live with Reji again. Memories of those years were too painful. Reji did not beat me, nor did he drink or have affairs. However, only women who have gone through the torture of mental and emotional abuse can understand that psychological battering can sometimes be far worse than physical blows. Being a Christian, I struggled with the idea of divorce for a whole year. Having had a strict Christian upbringing and knowing that in the book of Malachi, God says, "I hate divorce," the very word "divorce" seemed hateful to me. On the other hand, as long as I remained Reji's wife, even if only in name, I would always be haunted by the past.

Two years later, I decided to file for divorce. Not once had Reji come to see us. Even after he received the papers, there was no communication from him. But, he did not fight my petition; it made everything easier when he attended the court hearings and even agreed to pay child support for Mathew. We were soon divorced.

I felt deeply saddened. What had turned Reji into such a hostile human being? Nobody turns into such a closed person by chance. Why had I not been able to win him over with love? He had never wanted my love, right from the start, and that had made me feel like failure. However, a month after the divorce, I made an important decision. I realized that I did not want to burden my parents because of what had happened to me. Of course, they loved me and would have been happy if we had stayed on with them. But I wanted a fresh start.

I prayed a lot during those days and had often wept at the feet of Jesus. I put my life in His hands and said that I would go wherever He would lead me. In what must have been an answered prayer, in a Christian monthly journal, I suddenly came across an advertisement for a music teacher from a Christian International school. To cut a long story short, I got the job and my son was admitted into the school, at a much reduced fee. We stayed in a teacher's cottage and, since food and accommodation came with the job, I was able to save almost my entire salary (and they paid us really well). Things began to look really bright for us.

For the first time in a long time, we found happiness. Mathew's bubbly nature returned and he made lots of new friends. I was able to put up a wonderful musical for the school annual function and it got fantastic reviews. Not only did I upgrade my musical skills, but I enrolled for a couple of crash courses, one of them being writing skills.

Was it easy? Did I like being divorced? Not at all. But I loved the return of hope. I loved hearing the birds sing and there was nothing to equal the pleasure to see Mathew grow into a fine young man. He is 21 now and has a special girl in his life. I pray that God will always keep him on the right path. The strange thing is that the couple of letters I wrote to Reji went unanswered. I felt a lot of pity and compassion for him, but then, he had made his choice. And I have made mine.

Riya: *"Mine was truly a match made in hell."*

Even though I have been estranged from my husband for 10 years, I still look over my shoulder. My marriage, like most women in India, was arranged by my elders. I had absolutely no say in choosing who I married. Rahul had a big job in the UK and was looking for a well-educated girl with a sweet disposition. I guess I fit the bill. I had just completed my MBA then. Shortly after our three-day wedding, Rahul and I left for the UK, to start our new life together. Rahul had already found a spacious one-bedroom rental for us. It was a typical English house and I fell in love with it on sight. It had a little garden and I had already started picturing which plants I would grow. It took us a few weeks to settle in. Since Rahul had taken leave for the wedding, he began putting in a lot of extra hours at work. We hardly saw each other. Given that this was an arranged marriage, I was hoping that we would get to know each other better but that just didn't happen.

After about two months, Rahul informed me that he had invited a few colleagues home. I was very excited because I hadn't really met anyone since I had moved there and I was hoping to make some new friends. His colleagues were all men. One was Indian while the rest were locals. One of his colleagues, Jim, kept complimenting me on my looks, my Indian clothes, and my cooking— and this went on the entire evening. I was a little flattered, as Rahul hadn't said anything about any of my homemaking skills. Shortly after they left, the trouble started. While I was doing the dishes, Rahul came from behind me and grabbed my hair. He pulled me so hard that I fell onto the chair. He started yelling at me. He called me a flirt and a slut. I was shocked, as I had not anticipated his temper. He slapped me so hard that I was sure that I had lost a tooth. He asked me if I had wanted to sleep with Jim. He kept yelling at me. I started shaking. I was so afraid. He went into our bedroom, took my pillow and blanket, threw it in the living room, and shut the bedroom door. I spent the whole night crying. The mood hadn't changed the following morning. He didn't say a single word to me. When he left, I was relieved. He ignored me for a couple of days and I was fine with that.

One Sunday, while I was in the garden planning what I wanted to grow, our neighbor stopped by the fence and started chatting with me. He was a fatherly type of a man. He gave me advice on what to grow and where to get the best soil and garden equipment. I had hardly entered the back door, when Rahul grabbed me by the shirt and pulled me all the way into the living room. He started hitting me and then he punched my stomach. I doubled over in pain. Once again, he went for my hair and started yelling at me. He used foul language and accused me of sleeping with people while he was away at work. He asked me to get out of his sight. I locked myself in the laundry room. I cried. I spent the whole day there. When I heard Rahul go into the bedroom, I came out. I was so hungry but didn't eat, because I was so scared he would come out. So, I just went to the sofa and lay down.

Rahul's temper got progressively worse. He started hitting me often. He would always come from behind. He would pull my hair so hard and almost cause me to topple backwards. I hadn't spoken to my parents for months. We didn't have a landline and I didn't dare ask Rahul for his phone. Sex was a horrible and painful experience for me. Rahul seemed to get aroused by speaking filth. I felt so degraded and cheap. In my fifth month in the UK, I discovered that I was pregnant. Rahul was excited. He said he wanted a son. He went on talking about his "son" and what he was going to do with him. He treated me a little better during my pregnancy. Even though we could find out the gender of the child there, Rahul didn't want to, as he was sure it was a boy.

EVERY TIME ANOTHER MAN LOOKED AT ME OR GREETED ME, HE WOULD LOSE IT

Nine months later, we had a beautiful girl. Rahul was so stunned. He refused to carry our daughter. He didn't even look at her. I don't know why but I wasn't surprised. Rahul wasn't involved in anything. I shouldered the whole burden of looking after a baby, as well as running a home. I hated marriage but loved motherhood. Kia was adorable.

Rahul was still as horrible as ever. Every time another man looked at me or greeted me, he would lose it. We fought all the time. My pitiful attempts at defending myself would always earn me a few extra, harder slaps. I didn't care anymore because I had become so used to it. Once he called me while I was breastfeeding Kia, and I said I'll come when I had finished feeding her. I was so lost in thought that I never heard him come in. He pulled my hair and I almost fell flat on my back with Kia. Kia started screaming. I was in shock. What kind of sick person hits a mother who is feeding her baby?

It was at this moment that I decided to leave him. I knew I didn't want Kia to live in such a hostile environment. He was really a beast. I started talking about a family holiday to India. He ignored me. He didn't want me to cry to my parents and tell them about him. They were so far away that I knew they couldn't do anything. Two years passed. I didn't get to see my parents and hardly got to speak to them on the phone. Every time a man looked my way—in the supermarket, restaurant, or anywhere—Rahul would get so paranoid. I knew that as soon as we got home, there would be a bad fight, which would end up with me getting beaten. What I had realized about foreigners was that they will greet you, irrespective of whether they know you or not. But, I guess, Rahul hadn't figured this out yet. He thought I was enticing them.

One Sunday, Rahul got a call saying that his father had had a heart attack and we all had to rush back. This was what I had been waiting for—a chance to go back to India. I played the part of a concerned wife and took care of everything. Rahul was so busy making arrangements that he didn't notice that I had packed everything of value to me. I knew I was never coming back to him. I hugged Kia so tight. A two-and-a-half year of abuse was finally coming to an end.

As soon as we landed in India, we went straight to his home. His father had been admitted in the hospital, and Rahul got busy taking care of his father. On the third day of our visit, while Rahul was out, I took Kia and all my belongings and went straight to my parents' house. They lived in another city but nothing could stop me from going to them. They knew I was coming to India but they didn't know if I would visit them.

I reached their house at 6 am in the morning. My mother was so shocked but happy to see me. My father was also at home and we had quite a family reunion. I made them sit down and, in tears, I told them about my marriage with Rahul. My parents were shocked. Even though Rahul had never let me call them, he had called them once a month. I realized that he was trying to see if I had told them anything, which I hadn't. My parents went from shock to anger. My father called a number of our relatives. Within a few days, my parents' house was filled with my male relatives. They were waiting for Rahul to turn up, to give him a piece of their minds.

He didn't come. He didn't call for a month or more. He went back to the UK and called my parents' home. I had already contacted a divorce lawyer; he had already received the notice. He didn't want the marriage, nor did I. But I did want Kia to live a good life, so I demanded child support. He gave it. Not much, but he did. I went job hunting and got a good job. My parents looked after Kia, while I went to work. I slowly started going out and made a bunch of new friends.

All this had happened 10 years ago, and Kia and I haven't seen her father since. Mine was truly a match made in hell. I am so happy that I found a way out. At one point, I thought that I'd fall to pieces and would forever be stuck in that sham of a marriage. But I came out and have become stronger and bolder. I was 24 then, and I am almost 37 now. I have shared my story with a few close friends and in a few support groups for women suffering from such abuse. We give strength to one another.

CONCLUSION

These women have shared their stories, not out of spite or wanting to prove a point. These are stories of survival. Those who have shared them have done so, to give hope and a little nudge of courage to other women who believe they are trapped for life. There is no trap in existence which cannot be broken open by a determined spirit. What we need to understand is that, solutions do not fall from the clouds onto one's lap. Difficult decisions line the path of transforming one's situation. Some of these decisions may have worked out fine and others may have lacked wisdom. The important thing is that each one tried.

THERE IS NO TRAP IN EXISTENCE WHICH CANNOT BE BROKEN OPEN BY A DETERMINED SPIRIT

WHAT ABOUT YOU?

Once you are able to resolve your situation and live in freedom, do what these three women have done. Do all you can to share your story with other people. What you have received in such generous measure, you must now freely pass on.

EPILOGUE:

The End is Just a New Beginning

"If the numbers we see in domestic violence were applied to terrorism or gang violence, the entire country would be up in arms, and it would be the lead story on the news every night."

— Mark Green

*L*ily awoke to the sound of beeping machines. Clearly, this was not heaven but she had never felt more dead than she did just then. Her nose slowly opened up, as she took in the sterile environment. She was in a hospital.

"You woke up!" her mother's voice rang out, all of a sudden.

Lily hadn't seen her mother till then, but there she was, looking like she had seen the ghost of one of her long dead ancestors. She looked pale and small. Her tired eyes were clouded with worry and the tears welled up slowly. She looked hesitant.

"The doctors told me you had almost died. If Arpit hadn't brought you in, you would have been dead by now!"

At this, her mother choked and then, when she couldn't contain it any longer, she began to wail. Lily was stunned. Her mother had always been strong and strict, with her emotions well in check, and yet, here she was weeping, much like on the day her father had died.

There was an awkward silence, which was accentuated by the busy machines and her distraught mother. Maybe it was not fitting for the moment, but in response, Lily said the only thing she could think of:

"Is there any food, ma? I'm hungry."

The transformation was remarkable. Lily's mouth hung open, as her mother dried her eyes and jumped into turbo mode. *"My child needs food,"* was all she seemed to have in mind, as she opened up big tiffin boxes filled with all the food that was allowed by the doctor for now.

As her mother began to serve her, Lily's mind began to flood with old memories: her teenage years with her parents and her brother; the day she fell in love with the man who would become her greatest nightmare; the day Anant was born; the times when she had passionately loved her husband; the incidents when he nearly beat her to death; the very moment she had decided that suicide was her only option; the cobwebs…

"*Eat!*" her mother urged her.

Lily mustered up more enthusiasm than she really had the strength for, as she ate slowly despite the queasiness. She didn't want her mother to worry. There was silence as she slurped her soup slowly.

"*I have been praying for you ever since we rushed you to the hospital. It is only God who kept you alive,*" her mother said, with much conviction.

"*I don't know, ma. Maybe. I haven't thought of God for so long,*" Lily said, trying to change the subject.

"*Maybe it's time you started…*"

A calm silence settled over the room once more.

Lily's mother had much on her mind. For now, her mind was firmly fixed on her dragging her daughter back to the land of the living. Her wretched son-in-law could wait. For now.

<hr />

Lily's mother closed the door to the room and stepped into the corridor. Her eyes fell on him almost immediately. That was one of the things that she had liked about him before; his presence filled up the room and all eyes seem to automatically turn towards his handsome form.

Only now, she felt every pore of her being burst into flames. She watched, as the man who had driven her daughter to suicide, walked along the crowded hospital corridor as though he didn't have a care in the world. For a moment, her anger hung suspended in the air, like thick smoke.

Then, it happened. She didn't realize that she had marched forward and pushed him forcibly. The aghast looks of shock on the faces around her didn't seem to move her. She felt every bit of resolve for politeness melt away. She grabbed his shirt and banged at his chest with a ferocity that alarmed the crowd that had gathered to watch.

"Have you no shame!?! You treated my daughter sooo cheaply! You act like you have done nothing wrong, but look! She nearly committed suicide because of you! How dare you behave that way with my child, huhhh!?!" she yelled.

"Wait! One minute, please! I'm sorry! Please listen!" he stuttered, more embarrassed than ashamed.

"No!! Don't say one word! When I read her diary, I found out who you really are. GET OUT! Who asked you to come here??? I have already filed an FIR!" she screamed in agony as she charged at him, but the male nurses restrained her.

Arpit had an unreadable expression in his eyes. He was exposed. They finally knew who he was! These random strangers were watching him, some even angrily shaking their heads. He seemed to hesitate, trying to figure out his next move.

As Lily's mother was escorted away, she composed herself for a moment, turned back and said, *"Your son is going to be just like you. A monster. He is going to thrash his wife every day, till a few of her bones break. He has learnt all of that from you and he will use it someday."*

A slight murmur of assent went up from the crowd as she walked away. People moved away from him, like he had the plague. He heard someone say:

"My sister is married to a man like that. He is a devil!"

Arpit found himself acting like a cornered animal. It is true what they say: all things come to light, eventually.

~~~◇~~~

Lily and her mother got out of the car and walked in through their little gate. Anant came running from the veranda and hugged Lily tightly, not wanting to let her go. Lily was still a little weak and she softly patted Anant's head as he buried his face into her clothes. Thankfully, she had been making a quick recovery. They walked through the lush garden and into the house. It felt good to be home again.

Lily and Anant sat on the sofa as her mother went to the kitchen to make some coffee. It almost seemed like nothing had happened. Like she hadn't been abused for ten years. Like she hadn't been driven to the point of suicide. Like she was safe and taken care of, but without the history. She marveled at the miracle of life, the life she had been able to give her son and the life that had been miraculously restored to her. She couldn't help but notice now, how much she desired life. A full life. Despite the scars. It made her think about faith. Was there really more to life than what she lived out on her own? She lost herself in deep thoughts.

"Papa left you a letter."

Those words broke through her thoughts and rested on her mind slowly. A letter? That was very unlike him. She was always the one with the fascination for words. He had always preferred working with numbers.

"*Where is he now?*" she asked hesitantly.

"*He left. He is not coming back, I think,*" he said, "*I am so glad he is gone, mumma.*"

Lily didn't have the energy to chide her son just yet. There was time enough to teach her son to respect his father, no matter what his past was like. For now, Lily was free. And alive. She still had to read that letter.

She tore the envelope at the end and pulled out a lone piece of paper with sparse words spilled over it. It simply said:

Lily,

I don't love you anymore. I haven't for the longest time. Only today did I realize that I have been incapable of loving anyone. I realize now that I am a hypocrite. God would never condone what I did. I need to face off with the demons from my past and I need to change for my son. I don't want Anant to live like I have. I want him to be a good man.

I'm sorry.

Yours,

Arpit

APPENDIX A

Beauty for Ashes

"The world breaks everyone, and afterward, some are strong at the broken places."

— *Ernest Hemingway*

I too felt that I was a failure. I was quite convinced of it. I was unable to change my circumstances. I was enraged and I sunk in despair. I wept and cried out to God. If He existed, I pleaded with Him to come to my aid. God remained silent for almost two decades.

Do you feel that your sanity is on the verge of collapsing? Maybe you are consumed with feelings of self-pity, bitterness and hurt. Maybe your heart cries for justice, as you try to pull things together in your own desperate way. If frustration and confusion have stretched you beyond your capacity for endurance, know that you can rise above and emerge victoriously.

The phoenix rises from the ashes to give way to new life. Every death brings in its wake a new beginning. From amidst the debris of broken memories, a brand new life can emerge. But can all this be accomplished with broken dreams? Only one Person can make that happen.

I have often been told this: "You don't understand, Dr. Christie. My life has been like the bottom of a birdcage. You don't know what I have been through. It is easier said than done!"

Believe me. I am writing this from experience. Life hit me with unfairness many years ago, and I struggled for almost two decades, wearing a smiling mask and hiding the pain inside. I was walking on eggshells every day, trying to avoid another flare-up. I was manipulated and dominated, as my heart chased after a soulless, passionless relationship. While trying to sustain it, by denying the pain and chaos, I was focused on immediate survival. I was naïve and had constructed my life around my family, embracing it as my complete identity. But when betrayals and rejections came, I believed that I was dispensable and replaceable and ended up with shattered self-esteem. I felt betrayed by God Himself, as He seemed deaf to my pleas when my dignity and dreams were snatched away from me. I raised my fist towards the sky and cried out: "Does God really exist? If He exists, does He care?" My insecurity grew to such an alarming extent that I tried taking my life more than once.

Just when I was about to give it all up, the God of the Bible showed up. He met me on my death bed; I was dying of pneumonia, barely kept alive by a ventilator. In those stark conditions, God showed Himself to me and gave me new life. He transformed me, by becoming my therapist, counselor and best friend.

Wait a minute, you say. This is a book on Domestic Violence and now, all of a sudden, there is talk of religion! My expertise and knowledge is limited, as much as I would like to believe otherwise. I would like to tell you that following all the advice given to you in this book will erase your past, but I can't. Your past is what it is and it can't

JUST WHEN I WAS ABOUT TO GIVE IT ALL UP, THE GOD OF THE BIBLE SHOWED UP

be undone. If all else fails you, I wish to leave you with an earnest suggestion from my heart. My faith didn't remove my past but it shed new light on my experiences. I have come to a place from where I can look to the Heavens and give thanks for some of the most humiliating experiences I have ever been through. Meaning. Purpose. It is my desire that you find these.

COME WITH ME

Let me introduce you to my best friend. His name is Jesus. The great God who made heaven and earth, came in the form of a man called Jesus to this earth. He was born to a virgin in a little town called Nazareth, somewhere in what we now call the Middle East. He was never rich, a lowly carpenter's son that he was, but there was so much more to Him than what met the eye. He was different, had an exceptional intellect and could argue with the best of the scholars at age twelve. There is not much else that history tells of his life, till the time he turned thirty.

At age thirty, he performed his first miracle. This didn't prove that he was a holy man, but that He was the Son of God in the flesh. The Bible says that, through Jesus, God understood what it is like to be human. Previously, anyone could point a finger at God and say, "You don't understand what it's like to be human." So, God sent Jesus.

I love the part where the Bible speaks about Jesus being beaten and bruised for us. Not that I enjoy His pain, but that He understands what that is like. He is no longer a distant figure that sits on a throne somewhere and demands obedience. He went to great lengths to understand the pain of suffering and to carry the punishment of human sins on Himself. To think that He would make Himself vulnerable to ridicule, whippings and a crucifixion, is astounding. (For more information, you can read the following in the Bible: Matthew 26, 27; Mark 15; Luke 23; and John 19.)

Let me ask you a question: Would you willingly be beaten to understand someone else's pain? I don't think so. Honestly, neither would I.

Maybe the question that is running through your mind right now is: "Forget about Him feeling my pain. Why didn't He protect me?" To be completely frank, I don't know. I don't really have all the answers to the unspeakable situations in my own life. But I live every single day in the quiet knowledge that I am fully loved and I am at peace. Just to know that my pain is understood by a God who was abused for my sake, frees me somehow.

Why do you think I have been sitting with so many women night and day, holding their hands and trying to lead them out of their despair? Because He did the same for me; *He comforted me, so that I could comfort others.* Ten years ago, I wouldn't have believed you if you told me that

I would be helping people. God makes the most surprising things happen, when you give your worst nightmares to Him. Trust me. If you give Him a chance, very soon you won't be able to recognize yourself. Knowledge of His love can change you forever. It can give you a security you have never known before. You will stand in awe when you find out how precious you are to Him.

It Worked For Me

I want to tell you about my experience with God. I don't want to get into the details but I will tell you that for twenty years, my life was a complete wreck. Before I met this Jesus, I was angry with God, questioning what kind of God would ignore my pain. I had tried everything in the book but I was still desperate and eventually

> Knowledge of His love can change you forever. It can give you a security you have never known before

came to understand the futility of turning to people for help. Counselors provided temporary aid but the future stretched before me, long and desolate. I saw no means of escape and all I could do was watch my life deteriorate rapidly before my eyes—emotionally, physically and financially.

What changed me? He gave me new life, when I was so close to dying. To be honest, when I was admitted in the hospital with pneumonia, I was hoping I would die. I didn't want to go on. I had nothing to look forward to. I just saw my situation go from bad to catastrophic. It was at that minute that there was a supernatural presence in that ICU and I seemed to be surrounded by waves of love and comfort. "I am giving you new life," said an audible and clear Voice, over my labored breathing through the ventilator. The same Voice repeated the same thing again and again, and I felt like I was in some other world. I saw the Cross and the

Holy Blood flowing in torrents, and I could see every wrong thing I had ever done, getting washed away by that flow. I experienced an incredible lightness of spirit; it was as if a big boulder had lifted away to free me. This supernatural Presence engulfed me and I was feeling the embrace of the One, till I could breathe through my lungs and the ventilator was removed.

The Voice did not stop even while I was recovering. I heard this Voice say "Read the Word" again and again. So, I opened the Bible, which had been kept closed for so many years. "Do not let your heart be troubled, trust in God and trust in Me," said the Voice, and strangely, it seemed to be coming from inside me. I knew I was not speaking, so whose voice was it? For a moment, I thought I was hallucinating, but the Voice continued, "I will never leave you nor forsake you. I make all things new."

That last sentence was exactly what I needed. It was a chance to start life all over again; to put the nightmare behind me and begin afresh. I fell asleep and it was a gentle, peaceful sleep. When I woke up several hours later, I thought I had dreamt the whole thing. But the strong presence of peace and healing was all around me. By now, my spirit had begun to sing. I had not felt this way in a long, long time. I was giddy with joy, and though I was ill and weak,

I FEEL LIKE I HAVE THE MOST POWERFUL ONE—THE ONE WHO MADE ME BEAUTIFUL—AS MY CLOSEST COMPANION

I knew Jesus was there, holding out His hand. I took His hand and life has never been the same for me again.

More than anything else, I was satisfied knowing that God was always going to be with me, even when things might not go the way I want them to. Even now, I face tough

situations that really bear me down. But I am able to draw strength from the God who knows what I am going through. I feel like I have the Most Powerful One—the One who made me beautiful—as my closest companion. With His grace and strength, He helped me handle my messed up life. God used my hurts and pains, moaning and crying, to craft me into someone who can invest in the lives of others, to prove to them that no matter how painful the trial is, how deep the pit, there is still hope when God is in charge. He can make a beautiful vessel out of nothing.

A biblical story that continues to inspire me is the one in which the three Jewish boys—Shadrach, Meshach and Abednego—were put in a fiery furnace by King Nebuchadnezzar, because they refused to worship a statue of him. They said that they served the living God, who forbade the worship of statues. "We know our God can save us, but even if He chooses not to, we will not worship that statue," they said. This angered the King; he threw them into the fiery furnace and waited for them to burn. Imagine his amazement, when he found them walking around alive, in the midst of the burning flames. And to add to it, he saw a fourth man walking with them in the fire. God was in the fire with them.

This story moved me in a way I had never experienced before. God does not take away our trials but He is a God who walks with us. I was more convinced than ever that here was a God who willingly came down to experience our pain with us. I was able to draw strength from the God who knew what I was going through. I felt like I had the Creator of heaven and earth as my loving Father. Prayer, which was initially a monologue, became a dialogue with this Intimate One.

DREAMS: KEY TO A NEW DESTINY

Dreaming helps you move beyond life's trials; it is the hope that burns for something more than what we have—out of the ashes, like a phoenix.

Dare to dream with your eyes wide open. This dreaming is different from day dreaming. Nothing great is ever accomplished or established without someone having a dream. Every ocean begins with a drop of water, and every chapter of history starts with an event.

Sometimes, dreams die. I know from the pain of having seen some of them die. And for a while, I believed that dreams were for fools. But once God became a part of my life, He gave me the capacity to dream again and the new dreams were more far-reaching and enduring than the old ones.

Beloved, if you feel like all your dreams have died, I urge you to dream again. Let your dreams be resurrected through the power of God. Believe me, God will give you a life beyond all that you could have hoped for. You will be turned into a treasure worth beholding. If you think that this is what you are looking for, a God who will walk with you in good times and bad, then will you pray this prayer with me?

Precious Heavenly Father, thank you so much for helping me understand that there is a cure for my pain and that You love me unconditionally. I believe that You are going to do great things for me. I confess that I am imperfect and don't deserve to stand before Your Perfection. Jesus, I know Your blood was shed for my sake, on the Cross, to make a way for me to go to God freely. Forgive me and make me Your own. I accept You as my Savior and Lord. Come into my life. Change it and transform me into the beautiful one whom you made me to be. Father, I pray this prayer in the name of Jesus. Amen!

APPENDIX B

Prayers From a Crushed Soul

"They tell me Lord, that when I pray, Only one voice is heard;
That I'm dreaming, You're not there,
This whole thing is absurd.
Maybe they're right, Lord, Maybe they're right.
Maybe there's only one voice that's heard.
But if there's only one voice that's heard,
Lord, it's not mine, it's your voice.
I'm not dreaming; you are the dreamer.
And I am your dream."

— C. S. Lewis, *"Letters to Malcolm Chiefly on Prayer"*

*D*reaming is important. A dream will help you to move on and beyond—out of the ashes and up like a phoenix. Dare to dream. Your dreams are worthwhile.

Prayer is an intimate conversation between you and God. You might not believe in His existence or that He is good, given the circumstances of your abusive situation. But there is much healing in being able to speak the truth of a situation out loud, in the hope that you might be heard. After all, it is said that the truth will set you free.

Does prayer really work? Many don't seem to think twice about it when a plane is flying through turbulence or when in a bus, driven by a seemingly suicidal driver.

I don't know what your circumstances are like. Where are you in your journey? Are you in the midst of turmoil or in the process of healing? Perhaps you have chosen to stay and endure abuse because you've run out of options. Maybe you are scared that you might lose your children, you may not have any funds, or that no one will be willing to take you in. Maybe you have walked out, thinking your life will be better, and are instead finding yourself in a very deep pit all of a sudden. Right now is exactly when God can give you all you need. Many times, one needs to hit rock bottom before one can look up.

Writing out your prayers and saying it out loud has the power to change your circumstance. I am a firm believer in the cathartic effects of prayer. In this chapter, I have written down prayers for every situation that an abused person may go through, as she journeys through life. You may use it or modify it to suit your specific needs.

BEFORE THE "DECISION"

A person who has lived through much pain and hurt must heal first, in order to be able to make sound decisions. I am not trying to demean counseling or psychiatry, which are extremely useful tools that facilitate healing. But, having been through depression myself, I can honestly say that while seeking professional help from time to time can be beneficial, people's understanding, at the end of the day, is limited. More often than not, it takes divine intervention to heal a person completely.

Maybe you are toying with the idea of looking to God for help. Maybe you are not sure yet. If you think that you might want to give this prayer thing a go, why don't you try saying the following prayer out loud?

WRITING OUT YOUR PRAYERS AND SAYING IT OUT LOUD HAS THE POWER TO CHANGE YOUR CIRCUMSTANCE

Dear God,

I know for sure that you have heard my cries and have seen my tears and my deep emotional wounds. I ask You to release Your power in my life. You are the Healer of the brokenhearted. I fully believe that You set the captives free and bind up their wounds. Please come and heal my wounded heart. By Your love and power, remove the hurt and anger that I am experiencing. Please heal me, Jesus, of all those intimate wounds. It still hurts so badly. I offer you my heart. I ask You to set me free from any unforgiveness in my life. Father, You are my Creator. I pray that You show me who You really are. Surround me with Your love and empower me to move on, by Your grace and power. Jesus, heal me so that I can experience you. I pray that my past would no longer hurt, hinder, or destroy me. Help me to keep my eyes focused on You and help me to find the life that I have been looking for, in You.

In Jesus' mighty Name I pray. Amen!

WHEN DRAWING THE LINES

In your journey to healing, you are encouraged to evaluate your marital relationship realistically. Before evaluating it, calm your mind and give the complete exercise into the hands of Your Creator, who is waiting to walk with you at all times. The following prayer could help.

> *Precious Heavenly Father,*
>
> *I have come to You believing that You will guide me.*
>
> *You have said in Your Word that You will instruct and teach me in the way that I should go and that You will counsel me, as you keep your loving eye on me.*
>
> *I hold on to the promise that You will guide me and strengthen me and satisfy my needs. I trust You and thank You for this. Lord Jesus, You promised that You will send the Counselor, the Holy Spirit, who will teach us all things. When I sit in Your presence for counsel, I need Your Holy Spirit's guidance. Please help me make the decisions You want me to make, for good and not for evil.*
>
> *In the Name of Jesus I pray. Amen!*

THE HOLY SEAL

In your journal, write down everything that comes to your mind. Go through your life in detail: the past, the present and especially, the future. Do it slowly and let it take weeks. Begin your journal with a prayer every time, so you know that you have a God who watches over you while you write.

Deal with one stage at a time, and as you gain guidance and confidence, seal it with a prayer before moving onto the next stage. This exercise will help you decide what your next step should be to move on in life. Once you finish this exercise and are ready to make a decision, seal your decision with this prayer, which you may pray out loud. Let God open your eyes to see clearly all that you need to do.

> *Mighty Father,*
>
> *I love you and I know that You are here with me. I know You have listened to me and You know the efforts I have taken to assess my marital situation. Lord, I don't want to follow what I feel, but I want to do what You want.*
>
> *Please help me decide what I should do. I am confused. I have neither the wisdom nor the courage to walk either way, at this crossroad. So Father, I give my decisions to You and I wait for Your command.*
>
> *Your Word says that Your sheep hears Your Voice. Speak, Lord, because I am listening.*
>
> *In the Name of Jesus I pray. Amen!*

WHEN YOU MUST STAY

Never stay in the relationship just to adhere to a religious or cultural system of belief, especially one that falsely blames you for the abuse. After your session of evaluation and prayer, if you know that God is telling you to stay, turn once more to prayer. You need lots of prayer support at this time.

NEVER STAY IN THE RELATIONSHIP JUST TO ADHERE TO A RELIGIOUS OR CULTURAL SYSTEM OF BELIEF

> *Lord Jesus,*
>
> *You are my fortress, my place of safety and my shelter in the storm. Send Your angels for my protection. Please fight the battles that come my way. You know the dangerous situation I am in and You know the reasons that make me stay in this place. Never leave my side. Lord, protect my life, my children and my possessions. I am scared to fight my battles and I feel like giving up. The only reason I am not giving in is because of Your promise, that You will deliver me from this situation*

in Your perfect time and in Your perfect way. I will not curse or berate my husband because of Your command for me to love and forgive him. Please help me behave the way You want me to, in this situation. I commit my ways to You, Master, and I trust You to lead me step by step.

In Jesus' Name I pray. Amen!

WAITING ON GOD

If you are not sure what to decide even after the evaluation session and prayer, I encourage you to wait on God in prayer, for greater clarity. Sometimes, spending time in prayer and giving yourself more time to make a decision helps. Never rush or be in a hurry to do the first thing that comes to mind. Being impulsive will only complicate things for you. In quietness, pray these words:

My precious Lord,

I know You are working powerfully in my life and, when I am weary, You have promised to become my strength. You know, Lord, that I am in the middle of a raging storm. Help me be courageous, wise and determined. Hold my hand through this move to end the abusive relationship that has made my life a living hell. Let me not be blinded by circumstances. I need Your presence to guide me through this process. Speak to me clearly, so that I can make a decision that matches Your Will. I surrender my life, my children and my future into Your hands, Lord. Please have mercy on me and help me.

In Jesus' Name I pray. Amen!

WHEN YOU MUST LEAVE

If you need to leave and you sense that this is the right move to make, you need to be doubly careful and do it at once. There will be much that is uncertain, once you leave:

finances, friendships, career, etc. Asking God for guidance is crucial at this stage, but God is faithful to show you the right way out. Why don't you ask Him for his wisdom on how to go about leaving?

Heavenly Father,

As I tread unfamiliar territories, I want to hold Your Hand, so that I will not fall. I ask that You break down the barriers on this road to a new life. Guide me and restore me. I trust you to give me the peace and strength that You have promised. Help me to forgive. Set me free as You alone can do it. Give me the grace to come to You, in my helplessness and despair. Calm my fears. I know You alone have the power to make good things come out of bad situations. Help me to plan my exit from this situation, and come with me when I leave.

GOD SEES THE BIGGER PICTURE AND HAS THE BETTER VANTAGE POINT, HE IS ABLE TO GUIDE YOU ACCORDINGLY. DARE TO TRUST HIM.

I pray with confidence in Jesus' Name. Amen!

WHEN GOD SEEMS SILENT

Sometimes, it might feel like you are talking to a wall; that no one is listening. God might seem far away from you. You may get upset with God, thinking *"If God is really good, why do I hurt so badly? What did I do to deserve this life? When I am screaming at my loudest, why is God choosing to sit in silence?"* Let me tell you something: once upon a time I screamed at God, but He chose not to intervene. But, when He showed up later, at a moment when everything came together, I was filled with awe and wonder. God is always about timing. Since He sees the bigger picture and has the better vantage point, He is able to guide you accordingly. Dare to trust Him.

Even when you are feeling empty and disillusioned, dare to bow your head and whisper to Him.

> *Lord,*
>
> *I cannot stand the winds and the storms of my life anymore.*
>
> *Fill me with the Your strength. You are a God of majesty, power and grace. You spoke the world into existence and set the sun and the moon in place. You care for every detail of my life. Help me to trust You with everything. I am totally confused and devastated, and in my meagre understanding, I can grasp only bits and pieces of the things that are going on around me.*
>
> *Help me, O Lord! I am crying out to You for help. Teach me to find Your provision and shelter even in the midst of a raging storm. I humble myself under Your sovereign Hands. Teach me to walk with You, so that I do not miss my step. Help me, my God, as I am in desperate need.*
>
> *In Jesus' Precious Name I pray. Amen!*

GOD LOVES YOUR CHILDREN

Many times, an abusive marriage and divorce can be very harmful where children are concerned. But, God can give your children much understanding and wisdom, even in this situation. You need His Grace and Mercy. Put your arms around your children and pray over them, as you open your heart to God.

> *Lord Jesus,*
>
> *I thank you for the precious gift of these children, whom You have given to me. Precious Father, I want You to be the Lord of our home and I invite You to partner with me in parenting them. You know what is best for them. I release them into Your capable hands. Keep them away from abuse,*

*in their own lives. Put a hedge of protection around them
and guard them with Your angels. Let them become close to
You and know more about You each passing day. Use them
for Your glory and help them fulfill their destinies in You.*

In Jesus' Name I pray. Amen!

TO BE ALONE BUT NOT LONELY

Loneliness is common to all the victims of abuse, while
living with the abuser or after leaving the abuser. Do not
allow loneliness to destroy you. First of all, believe that you
are never alone. God is always with you. Trust that you are
unique and that you have something valuable and unique
to offer to the world. Cut out the criticizing voices of the
past from inside your head. Never blame yourself for the
abuse. Jesus knew what loneliness was like. On the cross,
just before he died, He cried "My God, My God, why have
you forsaken Me?" Don't waste time searching for new
relationships, but work on getting your wounds healed. But,
when your life feels empty at times, look to God for comfort
and companionship. Besides, being alone can be the best
solution while healing emotional wounds. Time and space
from people will quicken the process.

My loving heavenly Father,

*I am feeling all alone and, many times, I feel like there is no
one for me to talk to, laugh with, share a sad memory with
or to give me a hug when I need one. I long for someone to
tell me that everything will be alright one day. Bless me,
Lord, as I go through this loneliness, which pains my heart.
Please come right now and be near me. I invite You to invade
my life and take away my loneliness. I know that though
other people will let me down or leave me, You will never
do that. I am so grateful for Your love for me. I will always
remember that when the world seems cold and dreary, and*

*there is none to comfort me, You will always be there for me.
I trust my future into Your loving hands.*

In the name of Jesus, Your Son, I pray. Amen!

RESURRECTION OF DREAMS

Dreaming is important. A dream helps you move on and beyond—out of the ashes, and up like a phoenix. Dare to dream. Your dreams are worthwhile. If you feel that your dreams have gone to the grave, God is able to replace them with many, many more.

Everything is possible with God. Cheer up! You have a great future!

Say this prayer with me:

Father God,

I don't want to take one step without You. I reach up for Your hand and ask You to lead me in Your way, no matter where I am at this moment. You will make a path from where I am to where I need to be. Take me to the place where You want me to go. I don't want to run the race without You, as I will go off track. You are the light of my life and You illuminate my path. For all the dreams that I have been forced to surrender, give me new ones, Lord. Because I believe You are God. Nothing is impossible with You. Keep me close to You. I need You. Resurrect my dreams and give a new direction in my dead life.

In the Name of Jesus, I pray. Amen!

You can always write your own prayer. Draw it from deep inside your heart, where your pain resides. Sometimes, the best prayers are ones that rip straight from the heart. You can be candid with God about your needs. The reality and the intensity of your situation might find its best expression in prayer. Keep writing out your prayers, until one day, you will find yourself speaking your prayers out loud.

Why don't you try it? Write out a prayer and try to give shape and texture to your emotions.

APPENDIX C

An Overview For Those Who Support

"Capable, generous men do not create victims, they nurture victims."

— Julian Assange

No community, no society, and no country are immune to domestic violence. This family violence continues despite passing various Domestic Violence Acts and laws and setting up shelter homes and medical facilities. How can we stop this? Whose responsibility is it to stop this? Should the community not wake up to the horrible effects of abuse, and strengthen the support structures for the abused and the violated?

No community, no society, and no country are immune to domestic violence. This family violence continues despite passing various Domestic Violence Acts and laws and setting up shelter homes and medical facilities. How can we stop this? Whose responsibility is it to stop this? Should the community not wake up to the horrible effects of abuse, and strengthen the support structures for the abused and the violated?

This appendix is written for creating awareness among support groups like parents, pastors, church elders and so on, regarding the right way of responding to the horrors of domestic violence. Many NGOs and government organizations around the world have raised concern over the debilitating effects of domestic violence, but the Church that is supposed to respond compassionately to the cries of the victims and provide help and shelter has been silent because the church has not yet recognized the seriousness of this issue. Even the parents and relatives of abused women many times do not respond properly as they see only the tip of the iceberg the woman is suffering. Also, many Christians feel uncomfortable to discuss intimate partner violence as they feel it is a personal problem and hence it is better to ignore it than to deal with it. They are also not equipped to help the victims of abuse because of many misconceptions about what is acceptable, what is expected and what can be done. Even many religious leaders, who we assume must lead exemplary lives, actually indulge in intimate partner violence that is carried out in secret. This makes the issue all the more sensitive. Some even think that the Bible encourages such male chauvinistic behavior and this is another factor among the causes of family violence, even though the Bible condemns violence

THE CHURCH HAS NOT YET RECOGNIZED THE SERIOUSNESS OF THIS ISSUE

and encourages us not be silent towards the cries of another. This section will outline the biblical model of marriage and how the church (or any other support groups) should respond when evil and violence creep into that beautiful model.

BIBLICAL MODEL OF MARRIAGE

To get a better understanding of this sensitive issue, one should start from the nature and breathtaking activities of the Triune God who is the basis of all reality. The concept of Trinity, the one God who exists in three persons—the Father, the Son, and the Holy Spirit—is profound. The unity in diversity that exists among the three Persons of God is the starting point of the highest virtue, the love within any relationship. The perfect love that has existed among the three Persons of Trinity from everlasting was passed on to the humankind, the epitome of creation, in the Garden of Eden. The Bible indicates the unity in diversity that existed among them by the verse: "Let *us* make man in *our* image and likeness." God made both Adam and Eve in His very own image or resemblance and built the hardware for loving into their very being—the ability to love and to be loved. Matthew Henry remarks in his commentary on the Bible (Genesis 2:21–22), regarding the creation of the first woman from the side of the first man, "Women were created from the rib of man to be beside him, not from his head to rule over him, nor from his feet to be trampled by him, but out of his side to be equal with him, under his arm to be protected by him and near to his heart to be loved by him."

The beginning of human history holds a greater level of significance for our lives than we can ever imagine, as God made man and woman so that they can complement each other as one team. That is why Jesus gave importance to this part of history by referring to it in Matthew 19:4–6: "From the beginning, God made them male and female ... so [in marriage] they are no longer two but one..." Jesus pointed to the fact that God established a monogamous heterogeneous marriage relationship at the beginning. In the Garden of Eden, when Adam looked at Eve for the first time, he knew that she exactly matched him—bone of his bones and flesh of his flesh. They were both in the image of God, but she was different, made to compliment him, and they were unashamed and joyful. God intended sacrificial love and mutual submission to be integral to this exclusive relationship, lasting throughout their lives. In their world, which is marked by shared intimacy, both of them are free to communicate their thoughts, experiences, and emotions. The sexual union, that involves the husband and wife's total being, is not only physical but spiritual, and that is why it enriches the human spirit and does not degrade it. In such a relationship, neither is less than the other, as both were made in the image of God. The writer to the Hebrews says that marriage is honorable and its bed to be undefiled (Hebrews13:4). The garden relationship shows how God intended marriage to be—that a couple should live life with no trace of abuse, betrayal or manipulation.

A COUPLE SHOULD LIVE LIFE WITH NO TRACE OF ABUSE, BETRAYAL OR MANIPULATION

WHEN EVIL CREEPS IN

When sin and evil entered into this beautiful, intimate relationship, both man and woman drifted away from each other and God. In time, the Creator of the Universe chose to stoop down to the extent of entering this messy world and dying on the Cross to restore sin-laden humanity and the relationship He had with us. That is why Ephesians 5:25 says, "Husbands, love your wives, just as Christ loved the church and gave Himself up for her…" and again in verse 33, we read, "let each one of you love his wife as himself, and let the wife see that she respects her husband." God gave one command to the husband, to love his wife, and another to the wife, to respect her husband. This love and respect is part of the beautiful model. It is all about respecting, loving and submitting to one another (and it is not only wives, but all Christians are expected to submit to one another, verse 21).

ABUSE IS CONTRARY TO EVERYTHING THAT IS GODLY AND HENCE SHOULD NEVER BE TOLERATED

But if this approach to marriage is not followed, narcissistic tendency enters in and one partner tries to control and abuse the other by silencing them and violating their freedom and dignity. They can do this with a fist or with a bouquet. One abuse survivor said, "I felt shamed, defeated and trapped. The only love in my life I knew was from the man who kicked me and made me grovel under his feet like a puppy. I broke the chain of silence as I learned love does not hurt. I am no longer a victim but a victor. The scars that I bear do not pain me anymore." Authentic love does not devalue another human being; it does not silence, shame or abuse. It is every person's duty to give voice to the voiceless and restore families. Abuse is contrary to everything that is godly and hence should never be tolerated.

RESPONDING WELL TO VICTIMS OF DOMESTIC ABUSE

The history of domestic violence has been a history of silence and horror, and many families have borne the marks of violence. The body and emotions are damaged, relationships get broken, and the spirit withers. While some remain to tell their stories, some do not even live so that their stories can be heard, because their cry for help fell on deaf ears. The church should respond with the mind of Christ towards the suffering of abuse victims. Sometimes people who have never experienced violence or never been abusive towards anyone find it difficult to believe the story and the sufferings of victims or to feel compassionate towards them, and that makes the victims trapped, alone and scared. It is important for a church family to recognize that there are some families who are in pain and crisis. Sunday after Sunday, we might be meeting many abused women and children, who are silently sitting in our churches just to return to the abusive environment they live with because there is no one to care. From many pulpits, the notion of a happy Christian family that is sacred and ordained by God is preached, and this nostalgic image sometimes blinds us from looking into the plights of those who are suffering in their family. How I wish that every church should have a program to assist families in crisis and every pastor and every elder should learn the dynamics of abuse so that they can properly advise women who come to them for help. The church is the foremost place where many will turn when they end up in turmoil or when they need counsel.

Many clergymen use Scriptures to reunite the abused and the abuser because they find it difficult to differentiate between marital conflict and an abusive situation. Also, the manipulative husband might pose as genuinely repentant of his violent behavior and the woman might remain silent because of her fear and lack of social support and economic resources. The counselor or the pastor may hope that prayer might change the violent one and so they pray for him but fail to confront him. In one case, a lady was advised to go back to her abusive home as the whole church was praying for her and her family, and the husband was pleading for forgiveness. All may have prayed for her, but no one gave her shelter when her husband broke her bones. Later, she remarked painfully, "He broke my back, but I had to get right back into his home, forgiving everything." It is also difficult to imagine that a church-going Christian would kill his wife, but history tells us that this has happened again and again [16]. One pastor's wife revealed that he often used to grab her and pound her head against the wall, but people did not believe her because he seemed such a nice man, whereas she had (perhaps not surprisingly) been rather withdrawn.

Leaving an abuser even for a short period is extremely dangerous, and hence fear is permeated in every avenue of a victim's life—fear of the future, fear of losing her children, and fear of violence itself. Research consistently shows that abusers are more likely to kill their victims in the first two to three weeks after they leave than at any other time. Because of the secrecy, shame, and danger shrouding the abuse, it is very difficult for an abused woman to escape from her abuser. She may also be trying to find answers to questions like—who would help her? Would she land up on the street or would she get some job? Would the violence end someday? That is why she may well lie about an abusive action, perhaps explaining that she fell down accidentally when someone asks about the wounds on her body. She may try her best to conceal the abuse instead of disclosing it, keeping it as a deeply-guarded secret.

When somehow she musters the courage to open up if her motives are questioned and her story doubted, then she might stop disclosing and the thin window of opportunity to help her gets closed. It is better to be a part of the narrative of her story and to understand the extent of the abuse without accusing her. Already her abuser would have made her believe that she is the primary reason for all the abuse that is happening. An abused person is more likely to open up if she knows that the one who is listening will help and protect her while being confidential. It is also very important to win her confidence and make it sure that you will continue to provide support whether she listens to you or not. Support in the form of marriage counseling can be given only if the violence has stopped and the victim feels safe to talk freely without fear of retribution since many times counseling has proved to be dangerous, in the case of severe physical abuse. It is better for a pastor or an elder to start the conversation with her by first acknowledging her pain and asking appropriate questions that would not wound her more. She should be reassured that she does not deserve to be abused and that her long-suffering or being treated like a doormat is not Christ-honoring. We are not called to

THE IMMEDIATE PRIORITY SHOULD BE THE WELLBEING OF THE VICTIM

glorify suffering, but to apply healing balm to other's wounds like the Good Samaritan. A real shepherd would use the Bible verses to soothe her broken heart and to reveal how God hates violence and oppression while taking immediate steps to ensure her safety and the children's safety. Such a shepherd would never use the Bible verses to send her back into the abusive situation as God never intends anyone to live in abuse. In Ezekiel 34:22, God says, "I will rescue my flock, and they will no longer be abused." (NLT). However, unknowingly, many counselors have caused untold damage by advising the battered woman that marriage is inseparable (Mark 10:9) and that God expects her to forgive 70 times 7 (Matthew 18:22) and so she has to forgive and go back to him. Forgiveness should never be forced upon the victim as it only comes with time and maturity; the immediate priority should be the wellbeing of the victim. The impact of the family violence that happens behind closed doors is tremendous, and so we should have discernment and speak the heart of God.

One of my close friends, a Christian who suffered severe physical violence at the hands of her unbelieving husband, was advised by her pastor to demonstrate a more loving attitude to her husband and that her silent suffering of this mistreatment may result in his salvation—quoting 1 Peter 3:1-6. He even went to the extent of telling that, even if he kills you, it is okay as you will go to heaven since the Bible never advises you to leave him—basing this advice on Malachi 2:16. Many parents, relatives, and spiritual leaders care more about the reputation of the family than the suffering of the woman, and much effort is spent in concealing the abuse as they believe that it is a great achievement for them if they can join a broken family.

SAVING A LIFE IS MORE IMPORTANT THAN SAVING A MARRIAGE

Hence her scars go unnoticed and, with no support, she returns to her abuser, confused and wavering between the long-suffering that might be Christ-honoring, her marriage vows and the danger that hangs over her life and her children. Saving marriages should not be at the cost of the life of the woman and children. Saving a life is more important than saving a marriage, even though marriage is the most intimate of human bonds and intended to reveal the love of God.

Looking at abuse in the light of the biblical principles will help in the healing journey and the issue of forgiveness. Pastoral support is very much needed, to help the abused woman understand that God cares for her and to help navigate the woman through her healing journey so that she will not lose her faith. She might be struggling with suicidal tendencies or with other immediate and long-term physical consequences of the violence suffered. It is not only the pastor, but the whole congregation should function as a Good Samaritan so that the suffering one gets help. Only by our love for one another can we show to others that we are Christ's followers.

Imagine if every believer's home could operate as a temporary shelter home—because, if the abuser is violent, she needs some safe place to go, which the abuser does not know and where he cannot track her. Imagine if the Christian community could hold her hand, give her listening ears, and provide for her needs until she settles into a shelter or a job—like buying groceries, clothing, and providing transport for medical or legal help. How soon we could bring healing to her and empower her to face the challenges ahead! God wants us to bind up the broken-hearted and comfort those who mourn (Isaiah 61:1) because He is a God of compassion (Matthew 14:14; 23:37). The God of the universe is in the business of giving hope to the hopeless and in resurrecting dreams that have gone to the grave. He is powerful enough to bind up the heart that is broken, torn apart by loneliness and pain. Psalm 10:18 says that God will bring justice to the orphans and the oppressed so that mere people can no longer terrify them (NLT).

Every Church should organize programs and Bible study groups to discuss and condemn the prevalence of family violence and to understand how to support victims of abuse. The world needs men and women who will prayerfully, thoughtfully, impartially and immediately respond to the matter of family violence, without being judgmental, and who would bring the hope of the gospel into the lives of the wounded victims. I strongly believe that "Domestic Violence" as a topic should be part of the core curriculum of Bible college students and especially for health care providers. I repeat the quote from Martin Luther King, "the greatest tragedy is not the strident clamor of the bad people, but the appalling silence of the good people."

Let us not remain silent, but try hard to provide a safe home and environment for our sisters, daughters, and friends.

HEEDING THE WARNING SIGNS

Many such unfortunate marriages can be prevented if we give heed to some warning signs before marriage. Some couples rush too quickly from first-acquaintance to the marriage proposal or fall in love at first sight, thus creating a platform for entering into an immature marriage arrangement, failing to see the red flags. Some even live together before marriage or engage in premarital sex, increasing the risk for the marital breakup as this short-circuits some of the steps needed for a healthy marriage bonding. Along with such high-risk factors, an abuser has a typical profile, and many fail to watch out for indicators. It is better for the person who is entering into a marital covenant, or the parents or even the church leaders, to watch out for such warning signs and take some time to know him better before tying the knot.

Before listing warning signs, I would like to say that while some give warning signs, some potential abusers may be very adept at seeming gracious and at hiding a side of them that, after marriage, would become all too evident. So it is better to watch out for these signs before agreeing to marry and, if the warning signs start to emerge after marriage, it is wise to seek support from others (rather than allowing him to isolate you) and set boundaries, as discussed above, which may—God willing—help to prevent the situation escalating.

An abusive man unusually expresses a greater intensity of love, care, tenderness, and attentiveness early in a relationship, making the partner feel special and feel that she was the only one he was waiting for years. He may idolize her, putting her on a high pedestal and elevating her as the one to be worshipped. He may portray himself as a wonderful but broken machine that can function well only with the presence of his partner, causing her to pity him. One should never confuse pity with love. He will also try to isolate the partner from everyone else she was close to before meeting him so that she would always be dependent on him. He would show irrational jealousy and anger at other relationships that she has or develops, as he sees them as threats to him. He wants to be in control, either directly or indirectly, because he is insecure. He may force his partner to leave her job, or dress and cook only as per his liking. He would be having an inordinate sense of ownership, entitlement or possessiveness towards his partner. Many abusive men do not have a great friendship with other men in their work or neighborhood or, even if they have, it might be superficial.

If a person blames others for everything wrong that has happened in his life that is a huge warning sign. A potential abuser will disrespect his partner's personal boundaries since abuse thrives on disrespect. If a person disrespects elders, the poor or the disabled and passes negative comments about others' looks or clothes, it is not clear that he can be expected to be respectful towards his wife either. The foremost indicator is that most abusers would be very self-centered or narcissist in nature and they would not listen to other's viewpoints. They might intimidate others when they get angry or pass threatening comments or show abusive actions like raising his fist or punching or kicking doors or throwing things around. Some try to present themselves as a savior or rescuer, who is born to rescue his partner from her problems. These are some warning signs that can be watched for.

CONFRONTING THE ABUSER

Bible has called us to be peacemakers and peacemaking sometimes involves confronting evil face to face. Domestic violence is a great evil and a threat to the body of Christ which has remained hidden for many years, as no one talks about it even in premarital counseling. The phrase, "Break the silence," regarding domestic violence should be applied even to spiritual settings, and everyone should join together and confront abuse. God of the Bible is never silent on the issue of violence (Psalm 11:5, Proverbs 3:29, Isaiah 60:18), and Jesus confronted evil many times (John 8:1-11, Matthew 21:12-13, John 2:13-19, Mark 2:1-12, Luke 11:37-53). Isaiah 59:16 says, "God is astonished to see that there is no one to help the oppressed. So he will use his own power to rescue them and to win the victory." (Good News Bible).

THE CHURCH SHOULD HELP THE VICTIMS AND CONFRONT THE ABUSER

Though it is human nature to avoid potentially explosive situations, the Church should help the victims and confront the abuser. However, confronting the abuser and holding him accountable for his deeds is one of the most important and difficult avenues of intervention, because most abusive men feel that abuse is the right male response to a disagreement and that they are entitled to abuse their wives for their mistakes. They often make threats and false promises and, when confronted, may even cry, apologize, and promise that they will change. Since they are skilled in manipulation and lying, they can turn the story upside down, blaming the victim and making her appear as the reason for the whole thing. An abuser will often try to control the conversation, and direct confrontation can evoke threats, intimidation and abusive episodes. If the victim is still living with the abuser, the confrontation should be done in such a way that it does not jeopardize the victim's safety. Also, the confrontation should never be turned into a power struggle and, in case it turns out to be violent, it is better to have someone else with you. Normally the more receptive phase of an abuser would be immediately after a violent incident before he goes into the honeymoon phase.

Although changing an abusive man is hard work and frustrating, many men who were in violent relationships have changed when confronted. It is a challenge to distinguish between a man who might change and a man who might not. The one who might change is the one who can acknowledge that he needs help, rejects his cultural and sexist beliefs that spawn violence and understands that violence is not the right way to resolve conflicts. Such a person will feel real remorse for his actions, accept responsibility for his actions and will be accountable for his behavior. An abuser can change if he is truly born again as now his conscience is steered by the Holy Spirit and his desire for control and power is changed (2 Cor. 3:18). Those who might not change will make it clear that there is no problem with them and they need no help but claim that it is only their partner's problems that trigger the abuse. They would also take the view that only men should take charge as the head of the family and that the woman must submit to him in every way so that, if the woman challenges his headship, he has every right to use violence against her.

Since abuse is a multifaceted problem which is deeply woven into our social fabric, an interdisciplinary approach is required to respond to it. The assistance of the church should be offered to the victim and the abuser, along with other resources like Domestic Abuse Intervention Projects (available in only a few countries) and the help of physicians, shelter workers, psychologists, and lawyers. Domestic Abuse Intervention Therapy ensures that the abuser changes his attitudes and belief system before allowing him to go back to his family so that he would not revert to his old offensive ways. Since abuse is a product of traditions, habits, and internalized beliefs about the relations between men and women, the abusers need to be taught to confront their beliefs and attitudes like denial, justification, blaming and negative beliefs about women and marriage relationships, and to develop alternatives to abuse and controlling behavior. They also need to be taught conflict resolution, nonviolent problem solving, coping strategies and anger management. Such therapy will only be effective if the abuser takes responsibility for his actions and so it is better for such programs to have some connection to the justice system so that there are repercussions if the abuser is violent again. Some projects encourage group counseling for batterers as the group setting encourages men to share, trust and rely on one another.

If the abuser is not ready to change but continues to abuse the victim, criminal action can be taken. While some prefer therapy and mediation strategies that avoid the process of police intervention, arrest, prosecution and sentencing, others feel that criminal prosecution of the perpetrator is the appropriate response in order to protect the victims of domestic violence and to send a clear message that domestic violence is not acceptable. However, many cases of violence in the family setting pose serious difficulties as far as evidence is concerned, because such crimes occur in private. The victim may be the only witness and may refuse to testify against her husband or cooperate with the criminal justice process because prosecuting and sentencing her husband may, indirectly, also penalize her. If the victim continues to live with the abuser or has to meet the abuser often regarding the custody of the children, the abuser might threaten her, in order to persuade her to withdraw the criminal charges against him. If the criminal process ends up in acquittal, the victim may be in danger; but, if the process ends up in a prison sentence, though the victim may enjoy temporary relief, upon release, the perpetrator may behave even more violently. These are some of the reasons that make prosecution of the offenders very difficult.

However, the legislation has provided for a protection order or court order which protects the victim against further attacks or harassment. Such an order can be made if it is shown that it is probable that the abuser has caused and is about to cause harm. Such orders can forbid the perpetrator from approaching the victim, thus limiting his access to premises including his home even if he is the legal owner. Breach of such a protection order is a criminal offense, and the police have a right to arrest him without a warrant. Such an order, tailored to a specific situation, may offer a workable response to a domestic violence victim. Obtaining such orders is also relatively quick and inexpensive. Studies suggest that criminal proceedings, where the processes can be quite intimidating, do have a positive effect on the management of domestic violence [17].

Is Divorce Permitted?

Even after the repeated confrontation, if the pastor or parent finds out that the abuser has not changed, or when the relationship seems to have broken down permanently, then what should be the next step? Can the church permit the victim to divorce? Is ongoing abuse an appropriate and biblical reason for divorce? Christians have different views, and there is no consensus. I have listed the three main views regarding divorce:

1. The first view—no divorce ever view—says that there can be no divorce, on the basis of Matthew 10:6, "What God has joined together no man can separate," and Malachi 2:16 (NLT), "'For I hate divorce,' says the Lord God of Israel." However, Malachi 2:17—the very next verse says," 'and I hate a man's covering himself with violence as well as with his garment,' says the Lord Almighty." This passage was written during a time when men were divorcing their wives without cause, and so it was addressed to the man who was doing wrong, by tossing out his wife or hurting or mistreating her or using violence against her.

2. The second view—2 exceptions view—suggest that the Bible gives two conditions for divorce. Jesus acknowledged that adultery could come between marriage partners and gave this clause not as a command but as a concession for permitting divorce (Matthew 5:32; 19:9). The second exception or the so-called Pauline privilege gives another scenario (desertion) where divorce is permitted. If in a marriage, one partner becomes a Christian and the other one refuses to continue in the marriage, Paul says that the partner need not be bound in such circumstances (1 Cor.7:15,39).

3. The third view—3 exceptions view—lists abuse also as one of the exceptions where divorce can be permitted. One argument is that, when a person abuses or uses violence, he is no longer acting as a believer, and so he can be treated as an unbeliever. Since the abusive partner brutalizes his spouse making it impossible for her to remain in the relationship, forcing her to separate, it becomes equivalent to desertion like the Pauline exception. Some also argue based on the teaching concerning the rules about a woman sold into slavery

as a wife or concubine given in Exodus 21:10–11, "If he (the one who purchased the slave) takes another wife to himself, he shall not diminish her food, her clothing, or her marital rights. And if he does not do these three things for her, she shall go out for nothing, without payment of money." The proponent of this view argues that in domestic abuse, food, clothing, shelter, and love are lacking and so the abused woman can go free— that is, she is permitted to divorce. Another argument is that cruelty towards one's wife is equivalent to unfaithfulness.

God, in His mercy, will not allow violence and oppression to continue forever, but will intervene to execute His justice. To compel a woman to stay in an abusive marriage would amount to cruelty, and it is not clear that anybody has the right to do that. The bottom line is God is love, and we are asked to love and protect the weak. The church is uniquely positioned to be the protector and defender who will play a vital part in ending the horror of domestic violence across the world. Every believer should be equipped to help a woman either to set boundaries or to escape from an abusive situation and to confront the abusers so that he can either change or experience consequences. That is the biblical model of addressing oppression and abuse.

Divorce is a painful reality. Though undesirable, it becomes a necessary evil and should be considered as the last resort. While we believe in the power of forgiveness and reconciliation, we should also be concerned with saving a life than with saving a marriage. This section has opened up a "Pandora's box" regarding a controversial issue and, although I am against divorce like most Evangelicals, it would be cruel and unreasonable for an abused spouse to have no way of being free from this evil and suffering.

Which do you believe is more godly and biblical (let alone legal): to "aid and abet" illegal, violent abuse by joining the abuser in his insistence that the victim must stay with him, "submit" to her abuser, stay silent and put up with it? Or to confront the abuser and help and support the victim?

BIBLIOGRAPHY

[1] https://www.bjs.gov/content/pub/pdf/ndv0312.pdf.

[2] Pagelow, M.D., "Children in Violent Families: Direct and Indirect Victims," In S. Hill & B.J.

Barnes (Eds.), Young Children and their Families, Lexington, MA.: Lexington Press, 1982.

[3] Bowker, Arbitell, and McFerron, "On the Relationship Between Wife Beating and Child Abuse," Perspectives on Wife Abuse, 1988.

[4] Rosenbaum and O'Leary, "Children: The Unintended Victims of Marital Violence," American Journal of Orthopsychiatry, 51 (4), 692-699, 1981.

[5] https://www.misd.net/earlyon/files/Domestic%20Violence%20Toolkit.pdf.

[6] https://www.ncjrs.gov/pdffiles1/nij/grants/193416.pdf.

[7] https://www.unicef.org/media/files/BehindClosedDoors.pdf.

[8] https://open.library.ubc.ca/cIRcle/collections/ubctheses/24/items/1.0357257.

[9] Priscilla Schulz, LCSW "Change Among Batterers: Examining Men's Success Stories," A review of an article in Journal of Interpersonal Violence, V. 15 (8), August 2000, 827-842.

[10] Lewis B. Smedes, Forgive and Forget: Healing the Hurts We Don't Deserve, 2007.

[11] Lewis B. Smedes, Art of Forgiving: When You Need to Forgive and Don't Know How, 1997.

[12] http://lundybancroft.com/articles/understanding-the-batterer-in-custody-and-visitation-disputes.

[13] Elie Wiesel, Night, 2006, p.32.

[14] Peled, E., Jaffe P.G. and Edleson, J.L. (Eds.), Ending the cycle of violence: Community responses to children of battered women, Newbury Park, CA: SAGE, 1995.

[15] Hara Estroff Marano, "Divorced?" Physchology Today, March 1, 2000.

[16] Anne Horton and Judith Williamson, Abuse and Religion: When praying isn't enough, Lexington, 1988.

[17] Jolin A., "Domestic violence legislation: an impact assessment," Journal of Police Science and Administration, No. II, 1983, p.451.